The Boy

Marina Carr was brought up in County Offaly. A graduate of University College Dublin, she has written extensively for the theatre. She has taught at Villanova, Princeton, and currently teaches in the School of English, Dublin City University. Awards include the Susan Smith Blackburn Prize, the Macaulay Fellowship, the E. M. Forster Prize from the American Academy of Arts and Letters, and the Windham Campbell Prize. She lives in Dublin with her husband and four children.

by the same author

MARINA CARR PLAYS ONE
(*Low in the Dark, The Mai,
Portia Coughlan, By the Bog of Cats*)

MARINA CARR PLAYS TWO
(*On Raftery's Hill, Ariel, Woman and Scarecrow,
The Cordelia Dream, Marble*)

MARINA CARR PLAYS THREE
(*Sixteen Possible Glimpses, Phaedra Backwards,
The Map of Argentina, Hecuba, Indigo*)

MARINA CARR PLAYS FOUR
(*iGirl, Girl on an Altar, Audrey or Sorrow,
To the Lighthouse, Gilgamesh*)

ANNA KARENINA
after Leo Tolstoy

BLOOD WEDDING
by Federico García Lorca, in a new version

MARINA CARR

The Boy

Part One

Part Two: The God and His Daughter

faber

First published in 2025
by Faber and Faber Limited
The Bindery, 51 Hatton Garden
London, EC1N 8HN

Typeset by Brighton Gray
Printed and bound in the UK by CPI Group (Ltd), Croydon CR0 4YY

All rights reserved
© Marina Carr, 2025

Marina Carr is hereby identified as author
of this work in accordance with Section 77 of the
Copyright, Designs and Patents Act 1988

All rights whatsoever in this work, amateur or professional,
are strictly reserved. Applications for permission for any use
whatsoever including performance rights must be made in
advance, prior to any such proposed use, to
The Agency (London) Ltd, 24 Pottery Lane, Holland Park,
London W11 4LZ

No performance may be given unless a licence
has first been obtained

A CIP record for this book
is available from the British Library

ISBN 978-0-571-40020-1

Printed and bound in the UK on FSC® certified paper in line with our continuing
commitment to ethical business practices, sustainability and the environment.
For further information see faber.co.uk/environmental-policy

Our authorised representative in the EU for product safety is
Easy Access System Europe, Mustamäe tee 50, 10621 Tallinn, Estonia
gpsr.requests@easproject.com

The Boy: A Two-Play Theatrical Event was first performed on 15 September 2025 at the Abbey Theatre, Dublin, with the following cast:

Godwoman Jolly Abraham
Chrysippus Noah Behan
Oedipus Frank Blake
Queen of the Furies Jane Brennan
Moon Amy Conroy
Chrysippus Harley Cullen Walsh
Woman Zara Devlin
Haimon Eimhin Fitzgerald Doherty
The Shee Olwen Fouéré
Farmer Seán Fox
Oreone Ronan Leahy
Creon Seán Mahon
Laius Frank McCusker
Antigone Éilish McLaughlin
Thesus Abdelaziz Sanusi
Sphinx Catherine Walsh
Jocasta Eileen Walsh

Director Caitríona McLaughlin
Set Design Cordelia Chisholm
Costume Design Catherine Fay
Lighting Design Jane Cox
Composition and Sound Design Carl Kennedy
Video Design Dick Straker
Movement Director and Choreographer Stephen Moynihan
Voice Director Andrea Ainsworth
Hair and Make Up Leonard Daly
Assistant Director Éadaoin Fox
Assistant Lighting Design Jess Fitzsimons Kane
Assistant Sound Design Ultan de Stanléigh
Associate Video Design Jachym Bouzek
Fight Director Alan Walsh
Singing Coach Danny Forde
Casting Director Barry Coyle

For Dermot, William, Daniel, Rosa and Juliette

Characters

Oedipus

Jocasta

The Shee

Laius

Chrysippus

Heavy

Oreone

Sphinx

Moon

Creon

Godwoman

Polynices

Eteocles

Antigone

Ismene

Farmer

Theseus

Haimon

Woman

Queen of the Furies

Soldiers

Women of Thebes

Hundreds of Babies
four who speak

Setting

A fluid space

Time

Always

THE BOY

Part One

Act One

SCENE 1

Dinner party. Table linen. Cut glass. Food. Wine. Oedipus, Jocasta and The Shee sit at a long table, gowns on the women, black tie affair on Oedipus.

Oedipus There's only us, us and the stories we can spin. Believing in God is like believing in money. Fiction. All fiction.

The Shee You think so?

Oedipus No one's ever come back.

The Shee You think not?

Oedipus I know not.

The Shee Suppose I was to say to you there's more.

Oedipus More what?

The Shee More God. More mystery, more everything, that the world is vaster, stranger than you imagine.

Oedipus Go on then tell me one of your stories. I love a good yarn. How I got where I am.

The Shee Supposing I was to say to you, your wife is not your wife.

Oedipus You hear that darling?

Jocasta Wouldn't that be liberating?

Oedipus Have you divorced me on the sly?

The Shee Suppose I was to tell you that she was married before.

Oedipus That's hardly news.

The Shee Where did you get that limp?

Oedipus What do you mean where did I get this limp?

The Shee Don't tell me you were born with it.

Oedipus As a matter of fact I was.

The Shee Was he?

Jocasta How would I know? I wasn't there at his birth.

The Shee Really?

Jocasta Well obviously.

The Shee You're old enough.

Oedipus Don't mind her.

The Shee Did you know your father was a paedophile?

Oedipus That's enough. This evening is over.

The Shee Boys. He liked little boys.

Oedipus How dare you!

The Shee That's how it all began.

Oedipus How all what began?

The Shee The curse.

Oedipus What curse?

The Shee You do know you're cursed?

Oedipus You are one twisted individual.

The Shee I'm twisted?

Oedipus What is it you want?

The Shee If someone said to me, your father is a paedophile, I'd want to know why they said that. I'd want facts. Evidence. But you don't want to know and that makes me think two things. You know already. Or you think I'm a liar. Ask your wife.

Jocasta Ask me what?

The Shee You have a nice life?

Jocasta Does that bother you?

The Shee You don't want me upsetting it?

Jocasta You couldn't do that.

The Shee The first son.

Oedipus What about our first son?

Jocasta I think she's referring to my first son.

Oedipus How do you know about him?

The Shee Where is he now?

Jocasta I'm not discussing this with you.

Oedipus He died.

The Shee Very convenient.

Oedipus You're upsetting her.

The Shee You know about this son?

Oedipus Of course I do.

The Shee Then tell me this?

Oedipus What?

The Shee Your eyes.

Oedipus What about my eyes?

The Shee How did you go blind?

Lights.

SCENE 2

Enter Chrysippus, aged nine, looks around. Laius follows him in, watches the child as he looks around.

Laius Home sweet home.

Mixes a cocktail. Chrysippus watches him.

What songs do you know?

Chrysippus A fair few.

Laius You going to sing me one?

Chrysippus I want to go home.

Laius When the war's over.

Chrysippus When will the war be over?

Laius When I say so.

Chrysippus You own the war?

Laius I do.

Chrysippus This your palace?

Laius And you're my guest.

Chrysippus Any other guests?

Laius No.

Chrysippus No servants? Slaves?

Laius They don't count.

Chrysippus Where's your wife?

Laius Don't have one.

Chrysippus Am I your prisoner?

Laius Sing the song you sang at the games.

Chrysippus No. I'll sing a different one.

This is the oldest song I know. So old no one knows where it really comes from. My mother got it from the Sphinx, who learned it from the Minotaur but no one knows where the Minotaur heard it first.

(Sings.)
Oh silver wind
Oh golden night
Oh sleeping child
My heart's delight.
Oh green world
Oh yellow . . .

Stops.

Laius Are you tired little man?

Chrysippus A bit.

Laius Then let's get you settled.

And exit both.

SCENE 3

Enter The Shee. Stops. Listens. Majestic, Celestial Music. Golden light. The Shee looks up. Falls to her knees. Static, garbled sounds, horses whinnying, snorting, from above.

Voice *(female)* Laius you say?

The Shee The very one.

Voice He's not getting away with that.

The Shee Will you sort it or you want me to?

Voice What's the weather like?

The Shee Hot.

Voice Where is it?

The Shee Thebes.

Voice That shower again! And this Laius is he one of Cadmus's line?

The Shee Present incumbent.

Voice The King? I'll put manners on him. Outrageous. Who does the child belong to?

The Shee Bastard son of Pelops from that little river tart Axioche.

Voice Never heard of her. And why hasn't Pelops raised his army to get the boy back?

The Shee Because you won't let him.

Voice Why won't I let him?

The Shee Because he killed Myrtilus.

Voice Why did he kill Myrtilus?

The Shee Because Myrtilus tried to get off with his wife.

Voice And why did Myrtilus try to get off with Pelops' wife?

The Shee Because Pelops threw Oenomaus off the cliff.

Voice (*getting confused, irate*) And why did Pelops throw Oenomaus off the cliff?

The Shee Because he wanted to win the race.

Voice (*exploding*) What race? What bloody race? There's a thousand races! I'm supposed to be at a race right now!

The Shee Sorry sorry sorry.

Voice What the hell is going on down there? Done in with ye!

The Shee Hope you don't think it's my fault.

Voice Are you the best they can come up with?

The Shee This is the fifty-ninth year of my priesthood.

Voice Where have all the visionaries gone?

The Shee They don't believe in you anymore.

Voice A little insurrection is it? The clodhoppers getting notions?

The Shee They don't believe in anything outside of themselves.

Voice Make them believe! That's your job! Make them!

The Shee They want proof.

Voice Ah proof! Scumbags and your proof. I gave you everything! I took my lyre and sang you out of muck! Muck and the wing bones of the first angels! Look around you if it's proof you want! Look at the playground I gave you.

The Shee I don't doubt you. I've never . . .

Voice Fine you want proof? I'll give you proof!

The Shee No! No I don't want . . .

Voice You want torture and regret? You want suffering and pain? You want the Gods to go down? Disappear over the horizon like the August sun? Fine! we have places to go, we can go but not before we bring ye all down with us.

She's gone.

The Shee Can I just say? . . . Hello?

Bows to above, exits backwards.
Lights.

SCENE 4

Enter Jocasta and Laius in their wedding clothes.

Jocasta Is there always this many flies?

Laius Take off that stupid dress.

Jocasta I don't like you.

Laius laughs.

Laius Bet you've never kissed a man?

Jocasta Bet you I have.

Laius Who?

Jocasta My cousin.

Laius We're all cousins.
 But have you done the deed? A little shepherd? A runty little goatherd up on your mountain? In the summer? Cool you down.

Jocasta You're disgusting.

Laius Be better if you had.

Jocasta I know all about it. The men, the boys, my mother told me. Know all about the deer and the doe, stallions, rams, bulls, saw it all in the fields. Love. We know all about love up the mountain, hanging by the belly like swallows, I know all about babies, I'm not a child.

Laius Suppose you think you're stunning now I made you Queen?

Jocasta What's to be stunning about? Stink of the place, bitten to the scut by the midges.

Laius What do you want champagne and roses? You'll find me different to other men.

Jocasta So I heard.

Laius What did you hear?

Jocasta Look all anyone wants from this marriage is a son, keep the line going, keep all the land, the power, the gold, you know the deal well as me, keep it all in the family.

Laius And you say I'm not romantic.

Jocasta I'm romantic. In my mind, on my own, just not with you.

Laius extends a hand.

Laius You may kiss your groom goodnight.

Jocasta Don't be stupid.

Laius What did you say?

Jocasta I said don't be stupid.

Laius (*looks at her*) You're not on the mountain now. You're in Thebes.

*Laius extends his hand again.
She kisses it.*

Off you go.

Exit Jocasta.

SCENE 5

Enter The Shee. Stands there completely still, watches Laius.

The Shee Laius, spunk of Labdacus, Lycus, Pelops, Cadmus. Have I got the right punk?

Laius Who let you in?

The Shee I ask the questions round here. You stole a boy.

Laius I love the boy. The boy loves me.

The Shee You stole a boy. You raped him. We saw.

Laius Who's we? Mad bunch of hags up in the hills screeching to Orion. No one cares what you see anymore.

The Shee I should bite your head off but I'm under strict instructions. Here they are.

Takes out a huge scroll, unrolls it.

This from the flashing-eyed Godwoman herself. See her thumb print. That's the blood of immortals boy.

Music under this.

(*Reads.*) Laius, son of Labdacus, from the faulty and most dubious line of Cadmus, is from this pronouncement forward, forbidden congress with man, woman, child or any sad creature that walks the desolate blue orb. This judgement, on pain of rupture, will see the greatest curse we can bestow on his rancorous head and on the heads of any who follows him as issue of his blood and corporeal pelt. In the event . . .

Laius Ah would you get out of my sight . . .

The Shee In the event of mortal offspring let it be heard now and forever, that said offspring will be the sole and just cause of his father's death and demise. And curse of curses, when said Laius departs his temporal body, eternity will not abide his soul in our environs, for we take gravely and unforgivingly harm to the innocent and the weak. In short we pronounce, isolation for the remainder of his earthly sojourn and afterwards the lightless oblivion for his immortal shadow, penance unredeemed and unpardoned till the sands of time are done.

Yours et cetera,
The grey-eyed Godwoman, daughter of Zeus, year of the silver wind and the red horsemen of the heart.
Ruling 339633699963961836722ZED.

Laius Nothing new there from your flashing-eyed witch of the beyond. Isolation and oblivion from the cradle is all we know down here. Who does she think she's talking to? Who talks of the soul these days? Who gives a damn?

The boy is mine. I'd never harm him. Why would I?

The Shee I've said my say.

Gives him the scroll.

For your records.

Exit The Shee. Laius watches her depart. Tears parchment in two, sound to accompany, stamps on it, exits.

SCENE 6

Enter Jocasta with Baby Oedipus swaddled in purple. She sings a beautiful lullaby, same one Chrysippus sang. Laius enters, stands there watching and listening. Enter Chrysippus and Heavy.

Jocasta
Oh silver wind
Oh golden night
Oh sleeping child
My heart's delight.
Oh green world
And yellow grain
The purple yield

Of the falling rain.
And the amber corn
That is . . .

Laius Here give him to me.

Takes the baby, looks at him. A baby hand emerges from bundle. Hands the baby to Chrysippus.

Go on away with him now.

Jocasta What?

Chrysippus I can't.

Laius You know what to do.

Chrysippus I can't.

Laius On a tree.

Jocasta What? What tree?

Laius Put this bolt through his heels. See, like this.

Takes baby's heels.

Hold them tight and hammer the bolt through. Got that?

Jocasta goes to Chrysippus, tries to take the baby back.

Jocasta Just give me the child.

Baby cries. Laius hold Jocasta back. A struggle.

Get off me you!

Chrysippus is giving Jocasta the baby. Laius pushes him.

Laius (*to Chrysippus*) Would you go to be damned!

Baby wailing. Jocasta wailing, trying to get the baby.

Jocasta Give him to me. No!

Screams, struggles as Chrysippus and baby vanish out the door.

NO! NO! NO! What is this?

Laius Whoa! Whoa!

Jocasta What in the name . . .

Roars, wails, fights as he pins her down.

Laius (*to Heavy*) Would you ever stop gawking and hold her down you dunderhead!

Laius and Heavy hold her down as she fights and screams.

There's a curse put on me!
  He's a viper, a viper in the nest.

Jocasta You're the viper in the nest! Bring him back. Oh bring him back. Please, please. What're you going to do to him?

She makes it to the door, they wrestle her down.

Come back you red haired scut! CHRYSIPPUS! You rip! If you lay a finger on him I'll tear your head from your shoulders! I'll cut your hands off! You'll wear them round your neck!

Laius Are you listening to a word I'm saying? Told you! The curse! He'll kill me in my bed!

Jocasta I'll kill you in your bed!

Goes for him.

I'll kill you in your bed!! Bring him back! What's happening? What's happening here? What are you going to . . .

A wail.

Not Cithaeron?

Laius Get her out of here! OUT! OUT!

Jocasta Not Cithaeron! Not Cithaeron! Please not Cithaeron where they nail them upside down to the trees! I'll do anything I swear anything, don't harm him don't harm him.

Laius releases himself from Jocasta helped by Heavy, who is dragging Jocasta off screaming, howling, fighting tooth and claw.

Laius Knock her out. Give her some sort of remedy. She'll be grand when she comes round. Big hullabaloo about nothing. Women!

Storms off.
Lights.

SCENE 7

Cithaeron. Night. Shooting stars. Babies hanging from trees everywhere. Hundreds of them. Swaddled in white. Hanging upside down like bats. Swirling. Like a mobile over a nursery cot. Baby noises. Gurgling. Laughing. Whining. Crying. Score under this.
Baby O is the infant Oedipus, swaddled in purple.

Baby O Them the stars she was talking about?

Baby 2 Are you new?

Baby 3 Shut up I'm in agony with the teeth.

Baby 2 Not the only one teething round here.

Baby 4 (*grunting, a massive fart*) Excuse me boys and girls. That'll put manners on her. Let her clean that up.

A growl, several growls.

Baby O What's that?

Baby 2 The wolves. What's your name?

Baby O I don't know. Can't make out one word she says.

Baby 2 Mine's the same. Put years on you.

Baby O Where are we?

Baby 2 Didn't I fall asleep and when I woke wasn't I here.

Baby O Kind of nice being upside down for a change.

Baby 2 Not much difference. Mad world.

Baby O There you have it.

Baby 3 Never said a truer word.

Baby 4 Cradle to the grave just like that.

Baby O cries, wails, a heartbroken baby's wail.

Baby 2 What's wrong with you?

Baby 3 The bolt in his heels.

Baby 2 Ah the bolt in the heels.

Baby 4 We all have to contend with the bolt in the heels.

Baby 2 Don't cry my little pet.

Baby 3 You won't notice it after a while.

Sound of wolves louder, closer, babies wailing.

Baby 4 Here they come. Good luck.

Darkness, terrible sounds, build to height then diminish, nightmare soundscape. Silence. In the darkness a star falls. Baby O swirls alone. Enter Chrysippus with Oreone.

Chrysippus He's here.

Oreone What's that in his ankles?

Chrysippus So they can't run.

Oreone Have you ever seen a newborn running? Is he still breathing?

Checks.

Chrysippus The mountain falling down with them. Dumping ground. This is all they ever know. Stars, flooded fields, wolves.

Oreone You know what ye are in this land?

Chrysippus I'm not from this land.

Oreone Savages. Out and out savages. Hell wouldn't have yees.

Chrysippus Will you take him?

Oreone Don't have a choice do I?

Takes Baby O down from the tree.
Baby O cries in agony.

I know, I know, you're all right little man we're only trying to help you. Look at the state of his feet. He'll limp the rest of his life if he walks at all.

(*To Baby O, who is crying through all the above.*) We have it. Gone. All gone. You're starving. I know. I know. We'll find a nanny goat for you. And you're wearing purple. Only one house round here wears the purple. Am I right?

He turns around. Chrysippus is gone.

Just you and me little man.

He wraps the baby in his coat, exits.
Lights.

SCENE 8

Enter Jocasta covered in muck and blood, dragging Chrysippus by the hair.

Jocasta Which tree? WHICH TREE?

Chrysippus The Cypress. The big one.

Jocasta He's not there.

Chrysippus (*a wail*) I want to go home.

Jocasta He's not there! Where did you put him? What did you do with him?

Chrysippus I want my mother.

Jocasta You know what I'm going to do with you?

Chrysippus (*cries*) I want to go home. I want my mother. I want my dad. I want my mom. I want to go home.

Jocasta You think they want you home after what you've done?

Chrysippus What have I done?

Jocasta What have you done? You see that beam there? Your mother told me to get a rope and hang you from that beam for what you've done.

Chrysippus She didn't?

Jocasta She did! I'm going to hang you till you die. I'm going to hang you the way you hung my baby.

Chrysippus I didn't hang your baby.

Jocasta You did. You did!

Chrysippus I didn't I swear.

Jocasta You liar!

Chrysippus I didn't I swear, I don't, I gave him, I don't know what . . .

Jocasta (*shaking him, demented*) Where is he where is he where is he?

Chrysippus A man took him from . . .

Jocasta Liar! Liar! Liar!

Heavy (*who has entered*) That's enough of that.

Separating them.

Go on Chrysippus.

*He carries Jocasta off wailing.
Chrysippus looks after her. Looks out.
Lights.*

Act Two

SCENE 1

Eighteen years later.
  The Shee stands there. Looking out. Enter Oedipus, terrible limp, a crutch, one leg bandaged, dried blood on the bandage.

Oedipus Are you her?

The Shee I am.

Oedipus Can read the future can you?

The Shee Better still I can read the past.

Oedipus What's that supposed to mean? That's just nonsense that is.

The Shee (*exiting*) Good day to you young man.

Oedipus No look, I was at a wedding the other day and this old man comes up to me and says my father is not my father and my mother is not my mother.

The Shee Aha.

Oedipus And it felt true.

The Shee Aha.

Oedipus So I went and asked my mother and she starts wailing and says it's a lie, a big mucky lie.

The Shee Aha.

Oedipus Bawling her eyes out, beating the breast, so I went to my father and said, level with me now, and my father goes real quiet for a while, just looking at me and then he says don't be a royal eejit, if you're not my son you're no one's and he bet the lard out of the auld lad who told me

I was only a cuckoo in the nest. So here I am to see can you throw any light on the matter.

The Shee Aha.

Oedipus That all you can say? Aha, aha, aha?

The Shee Aha . . . And you think they're lying?

Oedipus I don't look like either of them.

The Shee They smell different?

Oedipus Hair, lips, hands, the way they walk. You ever feel you're living the wrong life?

The Shee No.

Oedipus That you're some kind of imposter? That you should be somewhere else, someone else?

The Shee You want to know who you really are?

Oedipus I do.

The Shee Not many do. You sure?

Oedipus Course I'm sure.

The Shee Don't ever go home again because if you do you'll kill your father and marry your mother.

Oedipus Are you mad woman? Kill my father?

The Shee You're not listening.

Oedipus And marry my mother? That's just sick. Like you mean marry her? For real? Like . . . bed her down? My own mother? How dare you! Do you think I'm a nutjob like you riding the devil by the full moon?

The Shee Would you ever calm down and listen to what I'm telling you?

Oedipus Disgusting! If you saw my mother, a lady, something you'll never be!

The Shee Spare me your love song to the mammy.

Oedipus You're perverted you are. I think I'm going to be sick.

The Shee Ye all want advice and not one of ye wants to take it.

Oedipus Call that advice? That's not advice! That's the evil eye you're putting on me, they warned me about you, filthy altar hoor prancing the lanes pretending you have an in with the holy shower above. No one has an in with the shower above, we're all just stuck down here together. That's my mother you're talking about. My mother.

The Shee Then go and marry her, leave me in peace.

Oedipus Don't let me ever set eyes on you again or I swear I'll kill you.

Oedipus storms off limping.

The Shee You can tell no one nothing.

Exit The Shee.

SCENE 2

Enter Jocasta with a handkerchief to her mouth, followed by Heavy with handkerchief to his mouth. Sounds of moaning, suffering, flies.

Jocasta (*looks out*) Why don't they burn them?

Heavy No one left to do the burning.

Jocasta The stink. Why isn't Laius doing something? Where is he?

Heavy On a bender.

Jocasta Warn me when he gets back.

Heavy My sister gave birth to a dead child this morning. No hands. A girl with no hands and a tail.

Jocasta Sick of these horror stories.

Heavy And the cows are having pigs, the pigs, goats, the goats, hares. End of the world.

Jocasta Tell them I'll have my dinner in bed.

And exit Jocasta followed by Heavy.

SCENE 3

Enter Laius and Chrysippus. Still nine years old. Laius throws himself down. He lays out food and several bottles of wine. Chrysippus watches him.

Laius Mad cow. Gall of her.

Drinks.

Filthy mane on her, squatting there combing her hair.

Drinks.

Smiling if you don't smile, telling me I should be dead by now.

Chrysippus looks at him.

You're going to die. Your wife's going to die. The plague is on your land. The Sphinx is here to stay. The sun won't shine till the blazing-eyed Godwoman reverses her judgement and that's not happening.

Drinks.

I'm a good king. A bloody good one. Is it my fault the crop is soup? The vines gone black? Them all dropping like flies?

Drinks.

Ah Chrysippus, Chrysippus, Chrysippus.

Chrysippus looks at him. Enter Oedipus on his crutch, limp, bloodied leg. They watch him approach.

Footsore and weary stranger?

Oedipus That's it now. If you had a drop a water.

Laius Help yourself.

Oedipus does.

You come a long way?

Oedipus Long enough. What's this place called?

Laius Don't know if it has a name, only a bend in the road. Have a proper drink.

Offers bottle.

Oedipus Too hot.

Laius Suit yourself. What brings you to these parts?

Oedipus This and that. You?

Laius The same. What's with the limp? Must be hard tramping the roads with that leg.

Oedipus Fierce personal in your comments.

Laius The girls, the women don't like it. Men either. Merciless if we're not perfect.

Oedipus Seen nothing perfect on this Earth yet.

Laius Where you from?

Oedipus The coast. Acorintha.

Laius Wild desolate country, wave, rock, mountain.

Oedipus Home is home.

Laius You on the run?

Oedipus No.

Laius What did you do?

Oedipus Nothing.

Laius Men don't run for nothing. The law after you?

Oedipus No law after me.

Laius What then?

Oedipus What's it to you?

Laius Stingy with your story. Bet you don't have one. Just trumping yourself up with mystery. Or you were tracking down the Shee?

Oedipus That why you're here?

Laius Did she parse your palm? Read the bones? Weave her spells?

Oedipus Put the heart crossways in me.

Laius She makes it up on the hoof. What did she say to you?

Oedipus She said I'll kill my father and marry my mother.

Laius You won't be the first. Don't mind the witch. She said the same to me one time too.

Oedipus That you'd kill your father?

Laius The other way round, that my son would kill me.

Oedipus Well obviously he hasn't, not yet anyway.

Laius Damn right he hasn't.

Oedipus Why's that?

Laius Why'd you think? Move in on them before they move in on you. That's my motto.

   Drinks.

Oedipus You killed him? Your own son?

Laius No one takes me down, no one. No babe in his pristine cot. Nor no filthy tea-leaf-reading hell cat like the Shee. No, not even the smouldering-eyed Godwoman herself can get the better of me. They say the Gods play with us young man, well now you can say you met the man who played with the Gods. And won. Have a drink.

Oedipus No.

Laius Go on.

Oedipus I said no.

Laius And I say you will you wandering pup.

Oedipus I don't drink with murderers.

Laius takes bottle, gets up, gets Oedipus in a neck wrestle, pours the drink down him.

Laius When I say you'll have a drink you'll have a drink. There's many would kill for a drink with me. Do you know who I am?

Oedipus (*struggling*) Get off me you with your filthy wine breath!

Gives him a belt of his crutch. Laius pauses, sways, looks at him, puts down bottle.

Laius You want to use weapons?

Pulls out a knife.

Come on so you little cripple, you little runt, come on hit me with your crutch again!

Dancing around Oedipus with the knife, stabbing the air around him.

Oedipus You want blood? I'll give you blood.

A vicious fight. Music. Both well matched, crutch and knife. They go at it. Laius draws blood. Oedipus gets the upper hand, gets the knife, a ferocious struggle. Chrysippus watches as Oedipus stabs Laius in a frenzy, throws down the knife.

Oedipus (*in tears, shock*) He started it . . . don't know what happened . . . he pulled the blade on me first . . . I've never killed anyone . . . this is, this is . . . walking along minding my own . . . why didn't you come to his aid?

Chrysippus looks at him.

He's not your father is he?

Chrysippus exits.
   Oedipus runs off limping.

SCENE 4

Enter Jocasta slapping flies off her arms, her legs, her neck. Enter Heavy, following her.

Jocasta Put him in the ground wherever he fell. Let him be his own mourner. Buried him years ago in my mind. Bury him every night in my lonely bed. There's justice in the world after all though it comes too late for me. Good riddance and may my dead baby haunt him in his grave.

Heavy They're planning a big send-off for him. Your father's coming.

Jocasta To marry me off again? Who's the next swamp king?

Heavy They're fighting it out below at the gates, beating the daylights out of each other.

Jocasta Who killed him?

Heavy He ran off.

Jocasta I owe him one.

Heavy The grieving widow.

Jocasta (*slapping her legs, arms*) Bloody horseflies.

Exit Jocasta. Exit Heavy following her.

SCENE 5

Enter the Sphinx gnawing on a leg. She looks up. A huge Moon sails across the sky.

Sphinx Ah moon.

Moon Any news?

Sphinx Orangutans to a man.

Moon Just wipe them out. Get it over with.

Sphinx That's what I said but your one.

Moon What's she blathering about now?

Sphinx Have to wait for this young fellah.

Moon What young fellah?

Sphinx Some young fellah has to marry his ma.

Moon Poor misfortunate jackass.

Sphinx Your woman ranting, who said this, who said that, who said the other, all boils down to the usual rigmarole. The Oracle says don't. The clodhopper says I will if I want. The Oracle flattens him, the clodhopper cuts out his eyes or the other clodhoppers cut them out for him, the clodhopper repents, the Oracle relents, everyone dies and they all live happily ever after until the whole malarkey begins again and they've rolled me out to sort it.

Moon The auld bitterness.

Sphinx Don't see the point. Clodhoppers are doomed. Let them enjoy their doom. Sing the whole way down.

Moon I had some great times down there but that wasn't today or yesterday. I'm away.

Sphinx Drown them in your silver flood.

Moon If they bother to look up.

Moon glides off. Sphinx sits there, gnawing and singing to herself in a language we cannot make out. Her voice is extraordinary. Same melody as the lullaby.

Whahemeee baradanomon
   Ohweeaspar atreygrah
   Saleeahahah arawm
   Xnoooooooo rooooooooo
   Fassingnyuoumnya . . . (*Etc.*)

Enter Oedipus. Sees the Sphinx, goes to back off terrified.

Sphinx Limp, dark hair, the Cadmean chin, you took your time.

Oedipus What world are you from?

Sphinx Get down on your knees.

Oedipus does. She puts crown on his head.

Congratulations. You're the new king.

Oedipus King of what?

Sphinx King of Thebes. Welcome home. You want me to cure that leg while I'm at it?

Oedipus Can you?

Sphinx For a small price.

Oedipus What's the price?

Sphinx A night with me.

Oedipus Will I be alive in the morning?

Sphinx No but you won't notice. I'm good at death. Fast. Lethal. Save you all the lamentations down the line.

Oedipus I'm used to the leg.

Sphinx Fond of your wound?

Oedipus Who I am.

Sphinx Is it my tail?

Oedipus God no.

Sphinx You're lucky there's an embargo on you. Go on, down the mountain and tell that pack of baboons they can stop killing each other for the throne. The Sphinx has chosen.

Oedipus They won't believe me.

Sphinx They will when I lift the plague.

Oedipus So that's the smell?

Sphinx A riddle before you go.

Oedipus I'm good at riddles.

Sphinx Name me the one species on this Godforsaken planet that doesn't mate with its own offspring.

Oedipus Humans.

Sphinx Horses.

Lunges. Gives him a savage maul of a kiss that nearly kills him. Tail, paws, wings, fangs involved, the works.

Good luck.

Exit the Sphinx. Oedipus on the ground, checks he's not missing anything, limps off like a drunk man.
  Lights.

SCENE 6

Enter Jocasta in a black dress and black veil. Followed by Creon.

Creon He stopped the plague or so he says.

Jocasta And I'm his reward? I'm not doing this Creon.

Creon He's the only one the barons agree on. You'll do it.

Jocasta Who is he?

Creon Little runt with a gammy leg. I'll be ruling alongside him, keep manners on him.

Jocasta You've it all sewn up haven't you? The land, the money, the power. Where's the love? Where is it?

Creon Half the taxes of this city goes to me. That's where's 'the love'. That's where 'is it'.

Jocasta Why should they go to you?

Creon He's fine and dandy about it now. You make sure he stays that way. Put that veil over your face.

Pulls black veil over her face.

Act like you're giving him something worth getting.

Exit Creon. Jocasta rips off her veil. Enter Oedipus after a minute. They stand there looking at one another.

Jocasta I'm no cradle snatcher.

Oedipus I'm no baby.

Jocasta What age are you?

Oedipus What age are you?

Jocasta You can't just walk in here.

Oedipus You're one of the perks of the job.

Jocasta What's your name?

Oedipus Oedipus.

Jocasta Oedipus?

Oedipus Means swollen foot. Does it bother you?

Jocasta The foot or the name?

Oedipus Both? Either?

Jocasta Not like I have a choice. You happy to be Creon's bottle washer?

Oedipus I'll sort out your brother.

Jocasta The big words. How you going to do that?

Oedipus I know all about controlling trumped-up Earls and Athelings. I know how these things work.

Jocasta Who are you?

Oedipus You've heard of Polybus?

Jocasta Polybus of Acorintha?

Oedipus That's right.

Jocasta You're his son?

Oedipus And heir.

Jocasta Our little swamp will hardly impress you.

Oedipus It'll do for now.

Jocasta Very sure of yourself aren't you? For the heir of Acorintha you look a bit rough for wear.

Oedipus Looking a bit rough for wear yourself.

Jocasta That an attempt to woo me?

Oedipus No. I'm not crazy about widows.

Jocasta What have you against widows?

Oedipus All the bad habits from the first husband. Have to be broken in again.

Jocasta Go back to Acorintha.

Oedipus I can't.

Jocasta Why not?

Oedipus Do you believe in prophecy?

Jocasta No.

Oedipus The Shee?

Jocasta Don't talk to me about the Shee.

Oedipus You've had dealings with her?

Jocasta Certainly have.

Oedipus So have I.

Jocasta What did she say to you?

Oedipus I'll kill my father.

Jocasta Do you want to kill your father?

Oedipus Not that I'm aware of. And I'll marry my mother.

Jocasta She said that?

Oedipus Perverted old witch.

Jocasta Don't mind her. That won't happen. She put a curse on me too.

Oedipus What kind of curse?

Jocasta On my son.

Oedipus They didn't mention you have a son.

Jocasta I don't. I had.

Oedipus What happened him?

Jocasta My husband put him on Cithaeron.

Oedipus Cithaeron?

Jocasta The mountain. Because of a curse from the Shee, the Oracle. The Shee said my son would kill his father so Laius had him nailed to a tree on Cithaeron. That's what they do with babies round here.

Oedipus Really? Well they won't be doing it anymore. I'm sorry about your son.

Jocasta If you'd seen him. The gab out of him and the little screeds of hair sticking up. Like a love song he was, a love song at dusk. I'd crucify my own mother to lay eyes on him again. My little son never killed his father. Don't talk to me about the Shee.

Oedipus You don't believe in her? In them?

Jocasta There's only here. Now.

Oedipus You don't believe we were meant to meet?

Jocasta No I don't.

Oedipus And when we die?

Jocasta Dirt. Bones. Dust.
I'm too old for you.

Oedipus I'll be the decider of that.

Jocasta Is that a fact?

Oedipus Women make too much of their age.

Jocasta Don't attempt to sweet talk me. Past all that.

Oedipus You haven't much faith in men.

Jocasta I have no faith in men.

Oedipus You never been in love?

Jocasta Never. You?

Oedipus It's for the poets. I was dreading meeting you. Thought you might be an auld hen or a bit of a heifer left too long out to pasture but it's like I know you. Or like when you're weary or hungry or just plain done in and all you want is your own fire, your own book, your own glass of wine in your hand, that's what you're like, drawing me in out of the road and the cold.

Jocasta You're a complete chancer. Little king looking for a kingdom.

Oedipus Isn't every man?

Jocasta You can do better than me. I'm not a good person.

Oedipus All sinners down here.

Jocasta Things happened round here. Things I'm not proud of. I went a bit mad for a while there after they took my son. Things happened.

Oedipus You want to tell me?

Jocasta Not now. Maybe not ever.

Oedipus We all have our secrets.

Jocasta Don't say I didn't warn you.

He goes to her.

Oedipus Jocasta. Great name. What's it mean?

Jocasta No one knows.

Oedipus Mystery woman.

Jocasta That's me.

Maybe a kiss.
Lights.

Act Three

SCENE I

Above. The flashing-eyed Godwoman floats on her throne, telescope in hand, veil over her face. Her dress flows over the stage, she surveys the place with a telescope, settles on scene below. The Oedipals at home. Two boys of fourteen and twelve play chess. A girl of ten dances around the room. Jocasta watches her admiringly with a babe in arms in a purple gown. Oedipus enters, interacts with his children. Romantic music. Idyllic, the light golden.
Enter The Shee, above.

The Shee He's gone and married her.

Godwoman (*telescope*) Seems a good match.

The Shee His own mother?

Godwoman They look happy. Which one is Antigone?

The Shee The girl dancing.

Godwoman Dance away girl.

The Shee What do you want me to do?

Godwoman Leave them alone.

The Shee What about the curse?

Godwoman Which one?

The Shee He killed his father.

Godwoman Did I tell him to kill his father?

The Shee More or less.

Godwoman Glad someone's doing what they're told. Ah yes, I remember. Laius. The boy. Where's the boy?

The Shee There he is.

Lights on Chrysippus hanging in the room whirling in his noose. Music.

Godwoman It happens.
What sort of king is he?

The Shee Egomaniac like the rest of them. Calls himself a liberal.

Godwoman Is he the one knocked the head off my statue?

The Shee And drove a road through your sacred hill.

Godwoman I can be liberal too.

Calls over her shoulder to an invisible minion.

Send in the Sphinx.

Lights down on above.
 Below. The children wander off. Jocasta sings to the baby. Same song she sang to the Baby Oedipus in Act One, same image exactly. Oedipus listens as Laius listened then. The quality of his listening. Jocasta clocks this after a while, breaks off her song.

Jocasta Oh silver wind.
Oh golden night
Oh sleeping child
My heart's delight.
Oh green world
And yellow grain
The purple yield
Of the falling rain.
Green the clouds
And white the throne
Soul the first
Enchanted . . .
What is it?

Oedipus Your voice. That song. What's it called?

Jocasta This old lullaby?

Oedipus Places you've never been in it, places you've never been but know you were. Shadows calling to shades.

Jocasta You're moody tonight. Just an old song a slave boy used to sing, one of Laius' slave boys in the long ago.

Oedipus What was Laius like?

Jocasta Hardly remember. He fades. He fades. Well made. Very proud of his physique he was. Vain as they come. Up on his horse with his entourage of horse men. Dark hair. Blue eyes. Wide about the shoulders. Like you.

Oedipus Like me?

Jocasta Haven't thought about him in years. Why do you want to know?

Oedipus No reason.

Jocasta Big day tomorrow.

Oedipus Yeah.

Jocasta Speech written?

Oedipus Nearly there.

Jocasta They've never had it so good.

Oedipus That's what I'll be telling them.

Lights.

SCENE 2

Enter the Sphinx. Music. She looks out. She blows clouds of black, breath amplified. The Moon sails in.

Moon Here again?

Sphinx How've you been?

Moon Not a soul to give the time of day to.

Sphinx It's lonely work among the living.

Moon Anything strange?

Sphinx Not a thing.

Moon Clodhoppers acting up again?

Sphinx Aren't they all meant to be gone by now?

Moon Heard something about that alright.

Sphinx Maybe just a rumour.

Moon Massive comet coming this way.

Sphinx They keep missing. Light me along this gorge.

And exit Moon and Sphinx.

SCENE 3

Fanfare. Music. Wild applause and cheering as Oedipus, Jocasta, Polynices, Eteocles, Antigone and Ismene enter dressed to the nines. Oedipus and Jocasta in their crowns and robes. They wave and smile to the crowd.

Oedipus (*to cheers, applause*) Thank you. Thank you. I thank you with all my heart for this wonderful day of celebrations to mark my fifteenth year as your king and leader.

We have come a long way together.

Many of you say this is thanks to me but I say it is thanks to you.

Together we have flourished.

Together we have rebuilt Thebes from a plague-infested swamp to this glorious city state that is the envy of nations.

They come and they marvel.

They marvel at our marble palaces.

Our cypress lined avenues.

Our stately homes.

Our magnificent library.

Our hall of justice.

Our goldsmiths.

Our silversmiths.

Our bronze foundries.

Our doctors.

Teachers.

Poets.

Musicians.

Our army protecting our borders from those who wish us harm.

Big cheers and applause.

We are the envy of the civilised world.

We are the kingdom of kingdoms.

It is said of Thebes, far and wide, that even the slaves have slaves and those slaves live like freemen.

Huge cheers.

We live in fortunate times.

The old savage Gods are gone and with them their old savage laws.

This is the age of man.

This is our era, temporal and eternal.

We are the makers of destiny.

We are the law.

We are the measure of all things now.

We are the new Gods and this is our Paradise.

Thunderous cheers and applause. He takes Jocasta's hand.

They say behind every successful man there is an extremely shocked woman.

She is my life.

Everything I have achieved begins and ends with her.

Kisses Jocasta, whoops and cheers from crowd.

My children.

The heir and future king, Polynices.

Polynices steps forward, waves, smiles. Cheers from the crowd.

The prince Eteocles you well know, the best young horseman in the land.

Huge cheers.

The two princesses.

Antigone, who loves to dance.

He lifts her up. She waves and smiles. Oohs and Aahs from the crowd.

And Ismene who has just cut her first tooth.

More Oohs and Aahs.

And promises to be as beautiful as her mother.

More cheers.

We have come so far together and with your blessing I will take you so much further.
  But enough.
  Turn on the fountains.
  Let the wine flow and the music begin.
  Enjoy this holiday and let no man speak of death today.

Takes Jocasta's hand, whole family wave and depart to applause and cheers.

The Shee And can a woman speak of death?

Oedipus turns. They all turn.

A sacred woman? Whose altar you've smashed. How dare you take from me what's mine?

Murmurs from the crowd.

My temple burned. My world is ashes. The Gods in ashes. Without them we are ashes. Dust and ashes.

Oedipus We've survived this long without your Gods. We've survived in spite of them. Flourished even but that's not news you want to hear.

The Shee I come with news from the Oracle and I'm afraid it's not good news.

Oedipus When did you ever have good news? When did your Oracle ever tell us we're doing fine? That we're not the scum of the Earth? That we're not damned if we do and damned if we don't? Your Gods hate us, they'd put us back in the caves if they had their way. Talking to the stones, parsing chicken bones, sitting on your triangle, smoke coming out your nether regions. Insult to the Gods to have you as their mouth piece. Insult to women to call you woman. There should be a law against you. I think I'll make one.

The Shee You can always tell the desperate man by the way he takes the woman down. I'm not your paramour . . .

Oedipus Perish the thought . . .

The Shee I speak only what the Oracle speaks.
 The sky darkens.
 Disease is coming.
 Famine is coming.
 Your children will die at your feet, the skin sliding from their bones as it was before.
 The flies.
 The rats.
 The hunger.
 And then the war.

Murmurs, growing perturbation from the crowd.

Oedipus I read the signs now. Not you.
 I decide when there's hunger, plague, war. Not you.
 I say where eternity begins and ends. Not you.

The Shee The vines are blackening and the herds sickening.
 The lakes and rivers sludge and sewer.
 Filth in the air.
 Filth from the skies.
 All lost unless you root out the murderer who lives among you.

Oedipus What murderer?

The Shee The murderer who's bringing this catastrophe on your heads and on your land.

Oedipus I said what murderer?

The Shee A bend in the road. A young man with a crutch. Another with a knife.

Sounds from the crowd.

Oedipus Arrest her. Arrest her now!

The Shee (*to the crowd*) Your king's an imposter. Well you always knew that. But what you mightn't know, your king's a murderer. A murderer who killed a man in cold blood.

Shock, disbelief from the crowd.

Yes, in cold blood he killed a Theban on Theban land.
(*To Oedipus.*) You didn't hesitate to take the life of another man. And if that isn't crime enough you didn't hesitate to take the life of another man on sacred ground.

Sounds of outrage from the crowd.

And there's more. Crime of crimes. The life you took, the man you so savagely killed was the former king.

Even more outrage from the crowd.

Oedipus The king?

The Shee The king.

Oedipus Laius?

The Shee Correct.

Shouts and wails from the crowd.

Oedipus Never! Never! I would never kill a king.
(*To the crowd.*) You know me by now. I live by what's right and wrong. The old woman's angry because I closed her temple . . .

The Shee Burned my temple!

Oedipus Yes I burned your temple, your feathers, your geegaws, your straw dolls, your books of black stinking magic because we have moved beyond your philosophy of fear. We measure things differently now. We have brains in our heads. Eyes to see. Reason and common sense to guide us. We have courts of law. We have moved beyond your cloak and dagger, smoke and filth, demented prophecy that can be read a thousand ways.

The Shee (*to the crowd*) This is the man you worship. This godless man who rules you now, who sneers at your beliefs, who desecrates all you hold precious, who thinks he's above the law, who in his arrogance believes himself a match for the Gods. He has brought the plague upon you. The Sphinx is on Cithaeron singing her siren song again and she'll sing it until your little king is brought to his knees and learns there are greater and more mysterious laws that rule our lives.
(*To Oedipus.*) You can't deny you killed a man.

Oedipus (*to the crowd*) Yes I killed a man. Long ago. A drunk. It was self-defence. He came at me from nowhere. I was unarmed. If I hadn't killed him he'd have killed me.

The Shee That drunk was Laius.

Oedipus You Liar!

The Shee And then you ran from the scene.

Oedipus (*to the crowd*) It wasn't like that. The man I killed. By accident. It was dusk. I was wandering, hungry, thirsty, nowhere to go, (*to The Shee*) because of you! You and your prophecy that wouldn't let me go home. This man was boasting how he killed his son. I saw red. An argument started, he tried to force me to drink and when I wouldn't he pulled a knife. It was over before I knew it. But that man wasn't Laius. He couldn't be. I would never kill a king.

The Shee And bed his wife? And take his crown and kingdom?

Oedipus I was given this crown. I came to you like a saviour. I, Oedipus, the man with the swollen foot, the blow in from nowhere, the cripple, the gammy leg, I, Oedipus wooed the Sphinx and turned back the plague single handed while you hid in your hovels. I'll find the man who murdered Laius. And when I find him I'll show him no mercy. I'll brave the Sphinx. There will be no plague. I did it before. I'll do it again.

The Shee These miracles are only given to us once.

Oedipus This woman has hounded my life with her poison, her pishogues, her lies, trying to keep me down, trying to keep you down.
　Arrest her.

Silence. The Shee looks out. Waits.

I said. Arrest her.

The Shee They know I only ever speak what's true.
　I've said my say. I leave the rest to you. We live in the middle of things. Mortal we're born, all destined to die, we must depend on the worst, expect everything and when misfortune strikes the one beside you, always remember it was aimed at you and barely missed. Your turn next time. As the wise man said, why weep for part of our lives gone wrong when the whole of life calls for tears.

Exit The Shee.
Oedipus looks out to deafening silence from the crowd.

Oedipus My people . . .

He stands there, hold. Jocasta comes forward, rescues him, takes his hand, smiles at him, smiles out at the crowd.

Jocasta My good people.
　Can I tell you a story about the Shee and the Oracle?
　How dangerous prophecy can be?
　How it twists the mind and scutcheons the heart and turns us from our better selves.
　Laius, your former king, my first husband, was driven mad by a prophecy.
　Many of you will know this.

Many of you will know his crime that led to the prophecy.
The theft and rape of a child.
And many of you will know this crime went unpunished despite the Shee's prophecy.
I was a young bride, a young mother.
Many of you will know I had a son with Laius.
A little boy I never got to name because of the Shee's prophecy.
Many of you know what that prophecy foretold.
There are no secrets in Thebes.
And all of you, all of you know, my son never got to fulfil that prophecy.
My infant son never got to fulfil that prophecy because he was nailed to a tree on Cithaeron.
He died there, an innocent babe, thanks to the Shee and her Oracle.
He should be here.
Not a day goes by I don't think of him.
How he suffered.
How long it took him to die.
Even still I wake astonished it wasn't just some savage dream.
That it happened.
That this city allowed it to happen.
That I allowed it to happen.
We can never allow this to happen again.
The Shee is a false prophet and I charge her with false prophecy.
I charge her with the murder of my infant son.
I'd like to see her nailed to a tree on Cithaeron.
No more prophecy in Thebes.
No more Oracles.
No more Shee speak.
My husband will find the murderer of Laius and let that be the end of it.

My good people, you know me of old, trust me now and trust your king. Put the Shee's wild talk of doom from your minds. Don't let her mar the day and our celebrations. Drink, dance, let your hair down. You are in the safest of hands.

Muted applause, muttering, discontent.

(*To Oedipus.*) Let's go. Smile. Wave.

He does. She does. And exit.
Lights.

SCENE 4

Music. Voice of Chrysippus from above.

Chrysippus Hello? Hello? Is there anyone there?

Enter Chrysippus. Looks out.

Hello? Hello? Please? Someone? I don't know where I am? Hello? I can't see . . . I don't know where I am. Please is there anyone at all? Hello? Hello?

Exit Chrysippus.

SCENE 5

Jocasta and Oedipus.

Jocasta You never told me you killed a man.

Oedipus I'm done for.

Jocasta It doesn't bother you?

Oedipus You know what? It felt right.

Jocasta What did he look like?

Oedipus It was dark. How would I know?

Jocasta Was there anyone else there?

Oedipus Why?

Jocasta Because if it was Laius and there was a witness.

Oedipus There was a child. A boy.

Jocasta A boy?

Enter Heavy.

Heavy A messenger.

Oedipus Not now.

Heavy From Acorintha.

Oedipus Acorintha.

Thinks.

Show him in.

Exit Heavy.

Jocasta What did the boy look like?

Oedipus What boy? Just a kid. His son. Red hair.

Jocasta Red hair? No. He can't . . . that can't be.

Oedipus No I remember, it was red, and it was long, down his back.

Enter Heavy with Oreone.

Welcome to Thebes stranger.

Oreone You don't know me?

Oedipus Oreone? Is it you?

Oreone The very man.

Oedipus Ah!

Embraces him.

How are you my old friend?

Oreone After all these years.

Oedipus Where have they gone? Can tell by your face it's bad news brings you. Well? Which of them?

Oreone Your father. Four days ago. I'm sorry.

Oedipus It wasn't me.

Oreone What?

Oedipus I didn't kill him.

Oreone Some might beg to differ.

Oedipus Why's that?

Oreone You broke his heart.

Oedipus We don't die of broken hearts.

Oreone Many ways to kill a man. And your poor mother, she won't bury him till you come home. All of Acorintha waiting for you to take the reins.

Oedipus You'll be waiting.

Oreone You want to kill her too? Your father died calling your name. If you'd seen him lying there so broken and thin, I want my son, I want my son, bring him home, dear God let me see my son.

Oedipus It's a curse Oreone, a curse from the Oracle. Don't ask me what I did to deserve it. An old prophecy handed down by the Shee that I'd kill my father and rape my mother. That's why I left and never went back. As long as either of them are alive I can't go home.

Oreone Yes you can.

Oedipus You don't believe in curses?

Oreone Only a fool doesn't heed a curse but let me tell you something now that can be told because your father is dead. Polybus wasn't your father.

Oedipus What makes you say that?

Oreone I mean not your real father. Didn't I give you to him myself and you a tiny babe. And thrilled they were to have you in that childless house.

Oedipus You gave me to him? How? Where did you get me from to give me to him?

Oreone I plucked you with these hands half dead from a tree on Cithaeron. A young boy led me to you. I brought you home to Acorintha. Your mother Merope heard the story and asked to see you. She'd just buried another child. She put you on her breast and you hung there for five years. No natural child was loved so well. They doted on you.

Oedipus But who put me on Cithaeron?

Oreone I don't know but you were wearing this.

Takes out an infant's gown.

Oedipus Purple.
That's our colour.
House of Thebes.
I was wearing this?

Oreone I've kept it all these years.

Jocasta takes the gown.

Jocasta (*to Oreone*) Tell me do you remember the name of the boy?

Oreone Don't know if he ever told me his name. A little red-haired chap.

Jocasta Chrysippus.

Oedipus Oreone. Leave us. Now.

Oreone What have I said?

They look at him. Oreone exits.
Silence. They look at one another.

Jocasta I stitched this gown before you were born. Only thing kept me sane, stitching and sewing up a storm.

Oedipus Yeah.

Jocasta To . . . to have you returned and taken in the same breath.

Oedipus I thought you were on my side.

Jocasta What side? There's no sides left.

Oedipus All this time, you the curse, you the prophecy. How could you not have known it was me?

Jocasta How could you not have? I swear I didn't.
I did and then I didn't and then I did again.

Oedipus What does that mean?

Jocasta Stray thoughts, that's all, stray thoughts I refused to think . . . once you were sleeping and I looked at you and I knew, for a second I knew, but it seemed too . . . too . . . the impossible come true, a mother weeping for her long-dead child in the dark, choking, trying to hide it from you . . .

Oedipus Now that we know we can say that we knew.
Days I'd look at you and say, yeah that's her alright. I've married my mother but then most men do. Why should I be any different? If I was annoyed with you or you were in one of your black moods missing your long dead son and I'd look at you, and then you were definitely the prophecy fulfilled or the curse or whatever. Then for months I wouldn't think about it. You were just my wife and all was fine and the kids and all of that until some evening, an expression on your face I'd catch, or a heaviness under your

chin, or something so maternal, like your stomach sticking out and then I'd think, yes she has to be my mother. But mostly, no, I didn't know except when I did, and when I did I told myself that's stupid, no one marries their mother. Life can't be that crazy or absurd, the shower above can't be that vicious or mocking. And then sometimes I just didn't care. I mean what does it matter? What are these laws? Where do they come from? Why can't you marry your mother or your father or your sister or brother. What's the big crime? It's all just sex. There's all sorts of theories about disease and congenital defects and insanity but I don't think that those who marry out are particularly sane or happy either. And well if you do marry your mother, I imagine you get away with more than if you married a stranger. She's your mother. She's bound to indulge you and maybe you can depend on her adoration the way you can depend on nothing else because she'll know you as an infant and at least have loved you unconditionally for those few weeks if not after or since. I mean you come out of her and all you're doing is going back in. Innocent really when you think about it like that. And if it's not bothering anyone why should it be a law or illegal, or maybe it's because your mother will get old before you and you'll have to nurse her and you mightn't want to go to bed with her anymore and maybe when she's a very old woman she won't want to go to bed with you, but you can lie peacefully together holding hands like those enormous tombs in the hills from the golden age. And you can maybe help her to die which you'd probably do anyway if you were a normal son and hadn't married her in the first place.

If I had a choice? If I knew you were my mother, would I have married you? Probably, as long as no one knew. Would you have married me if you knew I was your son? Probably. The attraction has never seemed perverse or excessive to me. No stranger than what any man wants from any woman in the dark. If I was asked I'd say our life together is satisfactory, for me anyway, good even, at times really something. Is that the way it is for others? I don't know. I've been with you so long what we do or don't do seems what's normal, seems what everyone else does, but I don't have anyone to ask about these matters because you see, on Cithaeron, all my life I've been waiting for the wolves to come. I know that mountain. I thought it was my own private nightmare but now I know it was always real. Cithaeron, that no man's land, heels bound, those sounds, the streams gushing, lambs bleating, frozen, choking, feet in ribbons, smeared in shit, piss, mucus, will she never come? What have I done? If I survive this I'll survive anything, I'll wreak such havoc, I curse you on the shooting stars, the tearing wind howling down the mountainside, and Oreone comes with his sheep, the silver bolt torn from my bleeding feet, my hunger soothed on a ewe's teat in the crook of his arm. And time races on and I defile everything I can defile and everyone. The thing about abandon, you never come home, not even if you fulfil the prophecy, live out the curse and all the curses, your own and others and the curse of the world and being here and it so short and the bit of whatever thing there's supposed to be that's not death and may be akin to love or hope or the thing that holds you here. That's gone or you never had it, not even by marrying your mother, not by killing your father, not by having all those children that are your sisters and brothers as well as your sons and daughters. Cithaeron cures you of all that or maybe Cithaeron just clarifies it. Living is just nailed to a tree, arse naked to the howling wind and no one coming ever, and if by some miracle they do come it really makes no difference now whether they take you with them or they leave you there because you've become the tree and the nails and the howling wind. It's your song, your lullaby, your anthem and I assume it's the same for everyone, ripped from the nowhere, friendless into the strange and the cold, always having to prove something, having to be someone, for what and for whom and for why this gale of the mind? This wind? This soul? This little time? These paltry years? why shouldn't we marry our mothers, take the little comfort we can because it's nowhere else to be found if even there.

Jocasta When I lost you I thought I would die too. But I didn't. And you didn't. And we have children now. We have to think of them.

Oedipus Am I not one of your children?

Jocasta You're not my son. You're not my son. I gave birth to you, that's all. I gave birth to you and lost you long ago. I've paid for your death, long and hard, I'm paying still, I've paid too dear for you to be resurrected like this. You're my husband. The father of my children and that's the end of it. No one can ever know this.

Oedipus They know. They know. The Shee knows and if the Shee knows everyone knows.

Jocasta There are no witnesses.

Oedipus What about that boy when I killed Laius? What about him? He must be a man now.

Jocasta There's no boy.

Oedipus I saw him, a red haired boy.

Jocasta You couldn't have seen him because that red haired boy is dead. He hung himself. Long ago.

Oedipus Who was he?

Jocasta Chrysippus.

Oedipus The one who put me on Cithaeron? Who gave me to Oreone? Who was there when I . . . No it can't be. Chrysippis? Laius's boy? Why did he hang himself?

Jocasta I don't know for sure but I think it was because of something I said.

Oedipus What did you say?

Jocasta He lied to me. He said you were alive and I said some things. You talk about Cithaeron. I was on Cithaeron too. I scoured that mountain for you. All I found were bones, scraps of clothes and when I came back down the mountain Chrysippus was there and I begged him to tell me and he kept lying and . . . and at the time I was glad, glad because he had taken you from me so I took him from Laius, but now I see him and what he needed, his long hair, the sunset in it, a quiet manner, very refined for a child, he was Pelops' son and he always said his mother was a nymph, and she may very well have been because there was something otherworldly about the boy, like he wasn't fully here, he had many songs, Laius loved him if he loved anyone and Chrysippus loved Laius and followed him everywhere and if he was there when you killed Laius maybe that's a good thing, to take him wherever it is we go, if we go anywhere.

Enter The Shee. Looks at them. They look at her.

The Shee You're wondering can you hush this up. You're looking for witnesses. There's me. There's the whole city and if that's not enough for you there's the Oracle herself.

Pounds the floor with her staff. Music.

Grey-eyed Godwoman I call on you now.

Listens.

Grey-eyed Godwoman it's time to return.

Listens.

Grey-eyed Godwoman they want proof, come to us now in our hour of need. Come down among us thieves of the world, come down and speak to your lonely prisoners of time.

Listens.

Chrysippus (*voice, faint, very far away*) Hello.

The Shee Hello.

Chrysippus Where am I?

The Shee Hello.

Silence.

Who is it?

Chrysippus It's blue, it's black, it's no colour at all.

The Shee Who are you?

Chrysippus She said, go hang yourself.

The Shee Who said?

Chrysippus Dark hair she had, she said my mother . . .

The Shee Are you Chrysippus?

Chrysippus Who is my mother? Who is my father? Who am I?

The Shee Are you Chrysippus? Laius's boy?

Chrysippus I remember the games . . . I sang there and . . . and . . . and . . . there was a palace and a baby I put on a tree. That's what he said the man who said he loved me. Was it long ago the man who said he loved me? His eyes . . . where is he? . . . he had a wife, a girl from the mountain and a baby and another mountain and a tree and a baby and I gave the baby to a shepherd passing through, fine upstanding man from Acorintha he said he was.

Will you take him?

Light on Chrysippus above.

And the songs the man who said he loved me sang many songs he got from the Sphinx who got them from my mother the river nymph Axioche and my father had an

ivory shoulder because some God or other had taken
a bite out of him from grief when the Earl of the dead
stole her daughter and kept her locked away among the
pomegranates but I think this was maybe a long time ago
and happened somewhere else when I moved and breathed
in all the colours of the light. And the man who loved me,
if I could see him again. He was a king one time of a city,
a faraway place in a wide green valley, olive trees and
cypress and herds and tombs from the dawn of the tribe
made from marble and moon gold and seven golden gates
in and out of his city, all the sacred roads and the horses
pounding the yellow dust and the woman, the girl from the
mountain, the queen of this city said a terrible thing and
I believed her. A terrible thing she said about my mother
and a terrible thing was said about my father, a terrible
thing concerning me. Even now I can't say it. So I got a rope
while the man who said he loved me slept. I crept from the
bed, from his arms and the beam in the hall of the palace
from that fabled place of long ago and there I am swinging
and I think I will swing forever. And the man who said he
loved me said I'd be the death of him, that the grey-eyed
Godwoman was jealous, jealous of our love and couldn't
bear our happiness, our ecstasy, our love, things like that
he whispered in the sheets. And I said no, I won't harm
the baby, we can't, and he said the baby should never have
been born, he said the baby is the curse the Oracle foretold.
And I said, but Laius all of Thebes knows it's me who is
the curse. No, my darling, no, never, if you leave me I'll die.
But I had to leave him because the mountain Queen said
that terrible thing to me. Your mother will never and your
father will never again and you are nothing, nothing to him,
nothing to me, nothing to no one. Sing the old song he said,
sing it, the one the Sphinx handed down in the time of the
silver wind, the time of the red horsemen of the heart, the
red horsemen who gallop by here wearing their hearts like
slabs of meat outside their chests. I met an old woman who
said they are the passion men who eat up the world. Ah

sing the old song he said, the candles, the goblet in his hand, the eyes flickering, the stars, the sky. And I say I don't want to but for you I will.

(*Sings.*)
Oh silver wind
Oh golden night
Oh sleeping child
My heart's delight.
Oh green world
And yellow grain
The purple yield
Of the falling rain
And the amber corn
That is your skin.
And the amber corn
That is your skin. (*Etc.*)

The Shee This is where you go blind.

Puts her hand over Oedipus' eyes, whispers an incantation. Chrysippus' voice from very far away, barely audible, singing the Lullaby. The Shee removes her hand. Oedipus bleeds from his eyes. Lights.

End.

NOTES

1. Lines for crowd scene. To be inserted as fitting. Mixed, garbled, hissed, whispered.

Go back to where ya came from.

Y'auld cripple.

Gammy leg! Gammy leg!

Murdered Laius!

Cutthroats the whole line of them.

Whole city glad to see the back of him.

The little pervert.

That's mad that is.

Don't believe it.

Big arrogant puss on him.

That's not right at all.

Can't have that.

Gammy pup!

Only a blow in.

Boo! Boo! Boo!

Slept with the Sphinx and all.

What can you expect?

Get outta here ya chancer ya!

Ya dooradan.

Ya trumped up no one.

All the same cutthroats going back to the time of the flood.

If it's not one thing it's another.

Bloody foreigners they've the country ruined.

There you go now.

That's the thanks you get.

Now for you.

Sure who is he at all?

They're all mad in Acorintha.

State of him.

And the young one has the inbred jaw they all have.

Look at the old wagon.

Prancing in their crowns.

She's a breeder I'll give her that.

Did you hear what I heard?

She's carrying a bit of condition.

Gone a bit chumpy round the chops.

Too much smiling.

They could wave a bit less.

Do you like the shoes?

Who the bloody hell do they bloody well think they are!

Boo! Boo! BOO!

2. *Chrysippus.*

The final monologue a huge ask for a child actor. This can be recorded/amplified/the child can mouth the words or perhaps just the image of him on high or swinging in his noose. The stranger the better.

3. *The song. Lullaby.*

Oh silver wind
Oh golden night
Oh sleeping child
My heart's delight.
Oh green world
And yellow grain
The purple yield
Of the falling rain
And the amber corn
That is your skin
And the amber corn
That is your skin.
Green the clouds
And white the throne
Soul the first
Enchanted home
The first cradle
Where all begins
The first cradle
Where all is grown.

THE BOY

Part Two: The God and His Daughter

Act One

Enter Oedipus with his Cadmean staff, blind, a head wound. A terrible bandaged leg. Burning heat. He hobbles and taps along. Enter Antigone with a bag. He stops.

Oedipus Where are we?

Antigone makes no reply.

Antigone . . . I'm talking to you. Where are we?

Antigone Same as where we were five minutes ago.

Oedipus What do you see?

Antigone Sky, rocks, mountain. You're bleeding again. Let me clean it.

Oedipus Have we water?

Antigone Not much.

Oedipus Bread?

Antigone No.

Oedipus You'll have to beg.

Antigone Beg yourself.

Oedipus The next farmhouse.

Antigone We have cheese but it's gone rotten in the heat.

Oedipus You know what's best?

Antigone Yeah yeah, never to be born.

Oedipus And second best?

Antigone Depart as quick as you can. We're going to die on this road.

Oedipus Sing me a song to shorten the way.

Antigone I'm not in singing vein.

Oedipus A story then.

Antigone You're the one with the stories.

Oedipus You know what I've been thinking about all day?

Antigone What?

Oedipus The way they sang Thebes into existence.

Antigone Sang?

Oedipus Yes.

Antigone How?

Oedipus Two brothers. One dug. The other sang.

Antigone Those old stories.

Oedipus Still. He sang. Amphion sang with his lyre. A gift from Hermes, his lover. Amphion sang and the stones piled themselves on top of one another and the walls rose and Thebes began.

Antigone You believe that?

Oedipus Don't know what I believe anymore. Where are we now?

Antigone Still on the road to Athens.

Oedipus I can smell the sea.

Antigone Good for you.

Oedipus What's wrong? . . . This too much for you? Traipsing around after your old da.

Antigone I don't see the point in any of this.

Oedipus You think I should've stepped aside? Handed over the reins to your brothers?

Antigone They have them now anyway.

Oedipus They're not ready.

Antigone And whose fault is that?

Oedipus You think I neglected them?

Antigone You see them as a threat. You always have.

Oedipus With good reason. They ran me out of my own city.

Antigone It needn't have been like that.

Oedipus You don't know what you're talking about.

Antigone We'll die out here. Am I supposed to bury you where you drop?

Oedipus Go back to Thebes. I don't need you. Go back to Haimon.

Antigone You don't like him?

Oedipus He's Creon's son.

Antigone And I'm Oedipus' daughter. I should be grateful anyone wants to marry me.

Oedipus It hasn't been easy being my daughter. I'm aware of that.

Antigone You must've known. In your marrow. It must've felt wrong.

Oedipus You know what feels wrong? I'll never see her again. And as for knowing. I didn't. Not till it was revealed to me.

Antigone Ah the Oracle again. So this is about the Gods? You and the Gods?

Oedipus Don't you feel them? They're here. They never left. Let me sit for a minute.

Taps, finds a slab, sits.

It must be getting dark.

Antigone Dusk coming on.

Oedipus Best part of the day. When I had days. When it wasn't always night in here. The garden. The olive trees. The pear. Navy Theban skies, the first stars. Nights of silver. Another Time.

Antigone I remember you dancing around the fountain with her.

Enter Farmer. Looks at them.

Farmer Lord almighty! Hup! Hup! Do you know where you're sittin' man? Do you want to be turned into a snake?

Oedipus Who are you? What is this place?

Farmer You never heard tell of this place and it famous the world over?

Antigone It's a ditch with a tomb.

Oedipus Who is buried here? Some God?

Farmer Ancient ones greater and older than any auld God.

Oedipus Who?

Farmer The Furies.

Oedipus The Furies? Here?

Farmer You're sittin' on them.

Oedipus gets up. Farmer examines him.

You can't see canten you not? Well you're standin' on Fury bones. The whole shootin' lot of them. The grey-eyed

Godwoman sent them down into the ground right here, long before your time and mine.

Oedipus The Furies? The daughters of darkness? The old Gods? The old religion? The ones with the beaks and the wings?

Farmer The very ones. Drink your blood and make a necklace from your guts. Athene banished them under. That's their grave. You may get down on your crippled knees and beg for mercy for desecratin' their final restin' place.

Oedipus What's this place called?

Farmer Colonus.

Oedipus Colonus?

Farmer Now you have it.

Oedipus And we're standing on the old bronze road?

Farmer What's left of it.

Oedipus Then I've arrived. This place is my destiny.

Farmer Destiny is it? Well we get all sorts comin' through here. Destiny how are you, what happened your eyes?

Oedipus Penalty from above.

Farmer Oh Divine Mother you're not himself are you? The wide boy murdered his da in cold blood at the crossroads? Some class of a king of the swamplands beyond in Thebes isn't it? Laius wasn't it if the auld memory serves me still? And then he went and married the ma. Shockin'! Shockin' altogether. That's not you is it? This blaggard went be the name of Oedipus on account of he had a halt in his canter. If you're the same criminal connivin' article we want no truck with you in Colonus.

Oedipus Theseus is your king.

Farmer You know him?

Oedipus I do.

Farmer A mighty king. He rules Athens and the whole of Attica, includin' this place which has been sacred since Time began.

Oedipus Not as sacred as it will be when they lay my bones here.

Farmer Like hell they'll lay your bones here.

Oedipus The Oracle said . . .

Farmer Ah the Oracle, the Oracle. Which Oracle? There's millins of them all contradictin' each other. No. This place is sacred because this is the very spot where Theseus went down to steal the Queen of the dead, none other than Persephone herself from the rotten green boned Pluto. But didn't Pluto capture Theseus on his rampage and fastens his backside to a bilin' rock and then doesn't the Furies lay into him with their talons and whips. Only the luck of God Hercules happened by on his travels and dragged Theseus from his scaldin' rock, left half his arse after him. But others says this place is sacred because the grey-eyed Godwoman sent the Furies down into their grave here because the Furies dared to cross her in a court of law one time. You see Orestes killed his ma because Orestes' ma killed Orestes' da and he had to pay her back. Then doesn't the Furies get all hot and bothered bayin' for Orestes' blood. But Athene says, no, it's grand to slay your ma if your ma has slayed your da. The Furies was havin' none of it. Blood crime is Blood crime they said and Athene was to the pin of her collar to round them up and herd them in here and lock the tomb with her golden chains. She changed their name and all, called them the Kindly Craythurs, but that didn't work aither. You can hear them shriekin' and tearin' at the clay and shakin' the tomb to its foundations if you pass by here on a new moon. Mad for blood. If I was you I wouldn't lay my bones here no matter what your fine Oracle says.

Oedipus Go and get Theseus. Tell him Cadmean Oedipus, King of Thebes is here to parlay with him.

Farmer So it is yourself? And king no more if the rumours goin' the rounds is true. They're sayin' your missus hung herself from the wardrobe door.

Antigone Who's saying?

Farmer All sorts of rumours comin' out of the swamps.

Oedipus (*to Antigone*) Don't mind him.
 (*To Farmer.*) Just get your king.

Farmer He's not a great one for the Parlayin', sooner split your head with an axe.

Exit the Farmer.

Antigone You knew we were headed here all along.

Oedipus Not really . . . only something was said to me a lifetime ago. I'd nearly forgotten.

Antigone What was said?

Oedipus That I'd meet my end at Colonus.

Antigone This Godforsaken field? I don't like this place. Evil air about it.

Oedipus Evil airs have hounded my days.

Antigone You're not afraid?

Oedipus Of course I'm afraid.

Antigone Can I ask you something?

Oedipus You can.

Antigone Suppose it wasn't the Oracle. Suppose you didn't have to kill your father.

Oedipus You think that hasn't occurred to me?

Antigone You brought it all on your own head?

Oedipus I could've walked away?

Antigone I've seen your rages.

Oedipus Are we talking about those vicious ingrates?

Antigone Your sons? My brothers? Yes we are.

Oedipus Pair of back stabbers. Dictating to me? Giving me the haunch instead of the shoulder at the table? They put me out on the side of the road.

Antigone The whole city asked you to step down.

Oedipus I invented Thebes. It was a rat-infested plague-ridden backwater when I came along. When I first met your mother she was covered in flea bites. You couldn't go outside the door without tripping over the swollen dead. Wolves running down the streets with human legs in their jaws, starving orphans dying in corners, the skies black with crows, the gates swinging on their rusty hinges, a river of sewer sloshing against the walls. I called off the Sphinx and the Shee. I scoured, I burned, I buried, I planted. I filled the granaries and stocked the fields. I built schools, a hospital, a library, restored the great temple. My city. I am Thebes. Without me you're nothing and that's what drives you all mad. This father killer, mother marrier is all that stands between you and oblivion.

Jocasta has entered. She listens.

Jocasta What're you raving about now? You look like a madman.

Oedipus I thought I'd seen the last of you.

Antigone How did you find us?

Jocasta It wasn't hard and him dirging his sob story all over the land.

Oedipus They said you hung yourself.

Jocasta And were you glad when they said it?

Oedipus I didn't believe it.

Jocasta No I didn't hang myself.

Oedipus Too greedy for life.

Jocasta And that's a crime in your book? Too greedy for life? Or is it only your life that matters? Your greed?

Oedipus I asked you not to follow me. I asked for once and for all to be left alone.

Jocasta I'd love nothing more than leave you alone but there's others involved here in case you haven't noticed. Do you have any idea what's going on since you started this mad pilgrimage? Your sons are an absolute disgrace.

Oedipus You reared vipers, how could it be otherwise?

Jocasta Why couldn't you have stepped down without this tantrum? They're killing each other. Eteocles has got it into his head he should be the sole king and won't share with Polynices. Creon setting them against each other.

Oedipus Well we know what Creon wants. What he's always wanted.

Jocasta And Polynices has gone to that lunatic Adrastus.

Oedipus Adrastus of Argos? The Mycenaean shower?

Jocasta And word is he's after marrying one of Adrastus' daughters and Adrastus is now backing him to descend on Thebes. Thousands of them, bringing in reinforcements from the Islands to mow the living daylights out of Thebes and trounce us back into the stone age.

Oedipus Good.

Jocasta Good? Brother against brother? Your sons?

Oedipus I don't want to hear another word about my sons.

Jocasta And the Shee screaming from the walls that it'll be carnage. That there won't be man, woman, child left alive and the victory will go to whoever has you on their side. How, I said to her, how can victory go to whoever has Oedipus on their side when the only side that fellah has ever been on is his own?

Oedipus The Shee said that?

Jocasta And now Creon and Eteocles have the army out scouring the roads for you. They're going to drag you back in chains if they have to.

Oedipus What exactly did the Shee say?

Jocasta The usual banshee speak.

Oedipus Tell me exactly.

Jocasta That Thebes needs you living or dead for victory. That whoever has you will win this war and all wars to come.

Oedipus She said that. Finally the witch says something that makes sense. I can go home? Rule again?

Jocasta Are you mad? They won't let you past the gates.

Oedipus Why not?

Jocasta You know why not.

Oedipus But I could save the city.

Jocasta They won't let you in. They're superstitious. Afraid. The old blood crime. The Shee says no. Dusk footed Apollo says no and the people can't bear the sight of you.

Oedipus They'd rather die.

Jocasta They would. But Creon is scheming to get around the Oracle. He wants to set you up outside the gates to have you on side to win. To have your bones when you're gone.

Oedipus All in my hands again. The wheel turns beautifully. Now they need me. Well they can need till the cows come home. Great Gods, sons of air and light, you've answered my prayers. I have borne patiently what no man should be asked to bear. Wound upon wound, my body in smithereens and my . . .

Jocasta Enough with the lamentations! Sick of them.

Enter Theseus and Farmer.

Farmer That's him there with not an eye in his head. Don't know who the women are. Swamp folk. Nothin' good ever came out of Thebes.

Theseus Oedipus.

Oedipus Theseus. You came.

Theseus Why wouldn't I? Your name goes before you. What road brings you here?

Oedipus A long and crooked one.

Theseus Your own crowd banished you?

Oedipus Word travels fast.

Theseus I want no trouble with Thebes. Enough cutthroats of my own to keep me occupied.

Oedipus I'll cause no trouble.

Theseus Who's she?

Jocasta Jocasta.

Theseus Jocasta.

Has a good look at her.

I think we're related way back. The mother's side.

Jocasta Aethra of Troezen. I grew up on stories about her. She's a legend.

Theseus The mother's the mother and it's not like you can choose her.

Jocasta The same could be said about the children.

Theseus What can I do for you Oedipus?

Oedipus I need your protection.

Theseus From who?

Oedipus My sons.

Theseus You kept them spancelled too long. You may loosen the rope or sons'll loosen it for you. Can't you sit down and break bread with them? Let the bile flow? Share the view at the top?

Oedipus Too late for that. There's a war coming.

Theseus So I hear. Thebes and Argus thrashing it out.

Oedipus There'll be sides taken.

Theseus I can't afford a war this season. Besides I've no quarrel with Adrastus at the minute.

Oedipus You'll be drawn in and whoever has me on their side is going to win. This war and every other war.

Theseus Says who?

Oedipus Says Delphi.

Theseus Apollo himself?

Oedipus Himself and no other.

Theseus That so?

Oedipus All I need is a plot to lay my bones in and a few fistfuls of your clay to cover me over.

Theseus You're not dying are you?

Oedipus We're all dying Theseus. Yes, my time is done.

Theseus So you want me to keep you safe till then? Bury you in Attic ground? Make some class of a holy shrine for the shower above? Are you saying if I agree to all that I'll win every war?

Oedipus I am.

Theseus You're going to be a relic? A sort of a God?

Oedipus So it seems.

Theseus The Shee said that?

Oedipus Tell him Jocasta.

Jocasta She gave me this deed.

Hands him parchment.

Dictated from the stars she said. The thumb print of the immortal God himself. Immortal ink she'd have us believe.

Theseus (*reading*) Very hard make rhyme nor reason of Phoebus Apollo's immortal ink. This could be read any way.

Oedipus Give it here. I know what the immortal ink means.

Theseus Then you know more than I do.

Oedipus When I was a young man I went to the Oracle.

Theseus The whole country knows you went to the Oracle. Your father, your mother, et cetera et cetera but what's that got to do with this?

Oedipus The Oracle also told me I'd meet my end at Colonus.

Jocasta First I've heard of this.

Oedipus You see the Gods always had a great plan for me.

Theseus What great plan?

Oedipus To make me one of them.

Jocasta Ara for God's sake.

Theseus To make you one of them?

Oedipus Exactly that.

Theseus Hould your horses, if anyone's becoming a God around here it's me.

Oedipus It's me they picked.

Theseus On my land?

Oedipus I didn't write the prophecy.

Theseus Didn't you?

Oedipus This place will be sacred and you'll have my protection because I'm buried in it. The marvellous will happen here because of me.

Theseus Well we do what we can to protect the legacy. I have to hand it to you. You're some operator. But you're forgetting one thing. This place is already sacred. The Furies are buried here.

Oedipus The Oracle says nothing about them. Gang of crazy auld ones. Who cares?

Theseus I care. And I wouldn't be messing with them.

Oedipus They're long gone. Forgotten.

Theseus I'm not so sure about that.

Oedipus Who prays to the Furies? Phoebus Apollo is our God. No one remembers them, if they ever existed.

Theseus Oh they exist. And you want to be buried on top of them?

Oedipus Doesn't matter what I want. The Oracle says it'll happen here and you can't best the Oracle. I tried and look where it got me.

Theseus Maybe you can't best it but maybe you can help it along.

Oedipus You're not a believer.

Theseus Look here life has taught me a few sharp lessons in my time. My daughter. My son. Taken on whims. My wife killed herself two months ago. My father jumped off the cliff because I forgot to raise the white sail on my ship that would tell him I was alive. I left the black sail hoisted and he throws himself into the Aegean with the grief because he thinks I'm dead and me snoozing on the prow. The litany goes on. The lessons continue. Seems I have to learn the same thing ten times. So to answer your question, I'm not a believer but I'm also not not a believer if you get my meaning.

Oedipus None of us gets to the exit without all the corners cut off us.

Theseus I can't just peg you in on top of the Furies.

Oedipus It has to be here or you don't get the benefit of these old bones. You don't win the war.

Theseus What war? I'm not at war.

Oedipus Not now you're not but you need to be thinking down the line. If you have me Athens and Attica will succeed when they come for you and believe me they're coming. If not today, then tomorrow and if not tomorrow then soon. Whoever has me carries the day. The Oracle says it and I say it.

Theseus I suppose I've nothing to lose giving you six feet of local clay to lie in. But you may bend the knee to the Furies before we crack their vault.

Oedipus I won't desecrate the old shrine as long as you take me in.

Theseus Alright, I'll send food. Tents.

Oedipus I need nothing except the tomb of the Furies and your protection. Thebes must not get me.

Theseus Thebes won't touch you. I'll put men surrounding the place.

Oedipus Thank you. Give me your hand.

Theseus I need no thanks.

Oedipus You won't shake my hand?

Theseus You know as well as me it's against the law to touch the tainted hand.

Oedipus Tell me Theseus, if a man comes at you with a knife do you stop to ask him, are you my father?

Theseus And herself? The mother is a different kettle of fish entirely.

Oedipus The mother is a woman like the rest of them.

Jocasta Some claim I knew him from the second I clapped eyes on him.

Theseus And did you?

Jocasta What do you think?

Theseus I think you'd be hard put not to sniff out one of your own.

Jocasta I know what you're wondering. You all wonder.

Theseus Love's a queer thing. Nothing queerer. That much I do know.

Farmer Shockin' that's what it is, shockin' altogether. Shockin'.

Jocasta And who do you love my fine shockable sir?

Farmer I love the right and proper way.

Jocasta Oh we have an expert on love in our midst.

Farmer I'm no expert on love but I'll tell you this much, my missus didn't pup me and tup me and yees can have that advice for free. Your poor son. The jammy eyed hamstrung dunce. Look at him! No mother worth her salt would let him outside the door not to mind stravagin' the highways and byways of the world. Now they all say it was the Oracle, that the Gods made yees do the humpbacked deed but there's common sense in it as well. Ever occur to yees that the Gods is demented? As demented as yeerselves? That maybe the Gods is not the Gods at all? And what we're dealin' with is a parcel of Demons that has got loose and locked the good fellahs up. That ye're backin' the wrong ones?

All look up.

Theseus A wild jealous bunch we're contending with no two ways about it.

Jocasta They should be barred.

Theseus But we may keep the right side of them for fear they flatten us.

Oedipus They've never needed a reason to flatten us.

Jocasta Merciless murdering tigers. Why should we carry the blame for this waking torment if every second of it was written like scripture before we drew breath.

Oedipus Someday someone will parse their meaning but it won't be today and it won't be us.

Theseus I'll have them bring provisions for the women. Who's the girl?

Oedipus My daughter.

Theseus Ah all the lovely daughters.

Antigone Ah all the impossible fathers.

Exit Theseus and Farmer and Antigone.

Jocasta So you're just going to wait here in this ditch till you keel over? You're going to let your sons go butchering on the battlefield when you could so easily stop it?

Oedipus I don't wish to stop it.

Jocasta You hate us that much?

Oedipus Hate is the first emotion and maybe the most honest.

Jocasta Then spew your hate. Spew it all over us.

Oedipus As you spew yours and call it love.

Enter Theseus with Creon and soldiers.

Theseus I have Creon here.

Oedipus This is what I was afraid of. Get him out of here. Now.

Creon No, listen, Polynices is coming with an army from Argos.

Oedipus Now you need me.

Creon Unfortunately we do.

Oedipus But you won't suffer me inside the gates of my own city.

Creon We can sort all that out later.

Oedipus You whipped up rumours about famine and plague to set the people against me.

Creon No rumours. There is famine, there is plague.

Oedipus When isn't there?

Creon You want every man, woman, child slaughtered?

Oedipus They've given their verdict on me.

Creon You're no king.

Oedipus That's right. I was a king. Probably the greatest king Thebes ever slapped the laurel on but I'm something much greater than a king now.

Creon The magic carcass is it? Should we get down on our knees and grovel at the sacred feet? The supernatural dispensation conferred by the mad cow Shee.

Grabs him.

You're a lunatic sir and you're coming with me.

A scuffle. Creon, Oedipus, Theseus. Soldiers involved.

Theseus You may leave him be Creon. I've promised his protection.

Creon He belongs in Thebes. Thebes made him, the rightful king from the loins of the old king and the whole stinking Cadmus line of us.

Oedipus Now you say it when it suits your purpose. I've moved beyond Thebes, beyond all of you.

Theseus Let him go. He's on my ground now. We'll have the benefit of the hallowed bones if hallowed they prove to be.

Creon Where's your loyalty? Your own city? Your honour?

Oedipus My honour is intact no thanks to you. You think to shove me into some hovel outside the gates so I can win your war for you? Tell them back in Thebes that I'm revelling in the carnage to come. Get him off me before I kill him.

Creon You malignant rancorous butchering no eyed mongrel! Outcast from the cradle. Even your own mother couldn't stomach you. She handed you over willingly enough. She can deny it all she likes but I was there. I saw her put you on the mountain.

Jocasta You saw no such thing.

Creon You know what you allowed. Blame Laius. The dead can't stand up for themselves and contradict the lies of the living.

Goes for Oedipus again.

Hated seed of child haters. Your father hated you, your mother hates you, your sons, your daughters and most of all the Gods hate you. You're no sacred relic. Your grave will be a scar on the land, cursed and luckless. Wherever this man goes will . . .

Jocasta You've said enough!

Creon This is madness.

Theseus He's sick, he's footsore, he's bone weary. Take your men Creon and go back to Thebes. You're needed there.

Creon (*to Jocasta*) You coming?

Jocasta looks at him.

Thick as thieves. Hard to say which of you is worse. I know what I know and I know what you've always known. Almost feel sorry for him.

Exit Theseus and Creon.
Silence.
Oedipus lies on the ground. Curls up. Jocasta looks at him.

Jocasta Let me wash the dirt from the sockets of your eyes.

Oedipus It's true.

Jocasta What's true?

Oedipus You nailed me to that tree.

Jocasta No matter how many times I tell you.

Oedipus I'm lame because of you. Blind because of you.

Jocasta You're everything because of me.

Oedipus You hate me.

Jocasta When you're like this.

Oedipus Where would we be without Mother's hate and Mother's pity?

Jocasta We should go back. Try and salvage something. We're not the first to discover it's all one senseless dream.

Sits beside him, takes him in her arms.

You're all done in.

Oedipus They should've left me nailed to that tree.

Jocasta I should've ended it that day too . . . I met the Shee on the road here. Sitting in a gully, pulling nettles. Isn't it great for you, she said, the eyes swivelling to the back of her head. What's so great, I said. Nearly over, she said, all your children dead.

Oedipus She said that?

Jocasta The end of the line. All your children dead.

Enter Antigone.

Antigone They've put up a shelter. There's blankets and cushions. They're bringing food in a while. Roast lamb.

Exit Antigone.

Jocasta Come and eat. A good dinner always helps. Then we'll ask Theseus for an escort back home.

Oedipus The Shee is right. The end of the line is what we deserve.

Jocasta You'd sacrifice us all for that bloody Oracle?

Oedipus You don't understand. You've never believed in anything.

Jocasta I believe in here. Now. Us. The children we made. I believe in plenty.

Oedipus They want me here. All my life I've gone against them, tried to second guess them. See where that has got us. Look at me. Dogs chase me, people back off, children cry at the sight of me. No one will shake my hand. It's time I submitted, time I washed myself clean of this filthy world. Time I washed myself clean of you.

Jocasta You can wash yourself clean of me after you've stopped your sons killing each other. After you've secured your daughters' lives and safety.

Oedipus You've no idea what I'm talking about.

Jocasta I know very well what you're talking about. Divinity doesn't suit you. This wandering anchorite nonsense. As if they haven't enough fuel against us. You're no God in the wings. You're a man, a man like any other. I should know, I gave birth to you.

Oedipus Go back to Thebes. Abandon me again. I'm used to it.

Jocasta The old stick. A thousand lifetimes would not make up for the loss of you. But when I lost you, I lost you forever. The man I married was not that wailing babe.

Oedipus Any other mother wouldn't live. Any other mother would've strangled the children from her own son at birth. Any other mother would have recognised her firstborn.

Jocasta You think too highly of other mothers while trouncing your own.

Oedipus What did you see that first time you saw me because you didn't see me?

Jocasta I saw a boy, a lost boy who'd be easy to love. What did you see?

Oedipus I saw a woman past her prime. I saw an opportunity.

Jocasta Better if you'd died on Cithaeron.

Oedipus Finally.

Jocasta All your life you've goaded me to say it. I didn't mean it. I swear I don't. Those years we had.

Oedipus Gone.

Jocasta We can't judge then by now. Why do you need to believe your life is more significant than anyone elses?

Oedipus Because it's mine and because it is. I have been marked for something different. My bones, my life, my memory will be sacred. They'll fall on their knees and beg for my blessing. They'll build altars to me.

Jocasta All this traipsing the land has unhinged you.

Oedipus My mind is perfect. I see what others don't see. The Almighty pattern and my place in it. I am the living example that they exist and that we won't survive without them.

Jocasta I've managed fine without them.

Oedipus Because I've carried your share of the guilt and the burden. I've carried your curse from my first breath and I'll carry it to my last.

Jocasta My curse? Mine? You cursed yourself the day you stuck a knife in your father's throat and well you know it. This is all just posturing. Fabrications to avoid that one true fact. You killed your father and in killing him you killed whatever was decent in me. And no Oracle, no prophecy, no dream of immortal rehabilitation can ever alter that or make it right.

Jocasta exiting.

Oedipus And what of your crimes?

Jocasta My crimes are many and I don't deny them. That's the difference between you and me. I know I'm damned.

Oedipus How dare you! I am not damned! I am the opposite of damned. I am about to become, to become . . . You wait. You'll see. When I sit on my eternal throne I will . . .

Jocasta Your eternal throne?

Oedipus Yes my eternal throne and I will pass such judgement on you.

Jocasta You already have. You have slathered my days in crucifying shame. There isn't one moment of my life I hold dear, one memory that's not covered in dung thanks to you.

Oedipus So finally we get to the root. The stinking vault I rummaged in.

Jocasta You rummaged gladly. The knowing upping the rummage ante.
 I'm going back to Thebes. Try and save my sons. My real sons.

Oedipus Jocasta.

Jocasta No!

Exit Jocasta.
 Oedipus stands there in the starlight and the moon hovering. Sound of singing faint, far away. Who is singing? Apollo? The Furies? Oedipus listens.

Oedipus Dorian Apollo, bringer of light, child of mortal Leto and Zeus, ruler of Time and men. Phoebus Apollo, bright sandalled guardian of Delphi and the first golden laws.

Lord of the high places, singing the heart stopping beauty of the world with your lyre, hear my useless prayer. I'm ready to go. Guide me down your blue stairs to blue black oblivion. Many my crimes. Many my cruelties, small and great, deceptions past number. Merciful prince of the divine, forgive. My father. My poor old father. I'm ready. Come.

Enter Chrysippus.

Chrysippus Are you the blind king?

Oedipus Are you the God?

Chrysippus They said to get you.

Oedipus Who said?

Chrysippus The Good Ladies.

Takes his hand.

This way.

Chrysippus leads Oedipus off as the Sphinx and Moon come on.

Sphinx And off he goes.

Moon He looks the tad relieved.

Sphinx What're you up to?

Moon Swanning.

Sphinx You drunk?

Moon A little merry.

Sphinx What's the occasion?

Moon The future.

Sphinx What future?

Moon When I crash back into them.

Sphinx Oh yeah.

Moon A homecoming.

Sphinx Balloons and fireworks.

Moon They won't know what hit them.

Sphinx Good luck with that.

Moon Not luck. It's physics. It's eternal return.

Sphinx I heard a rumour about you.

Moon No rumour. It's true.

Sphinx You're going nuclear?

Moon I am.

Sphinx Doesn't bother you?

Moon Only a bit of excitement.

Sphinx They're using you.

Moon On the contrary I'm using them.

Sphinx How so?

Moon The quicker they blow me up the quicker I get home and blow them up.

Sphinx Pass me down some of your moon wine.

Moon does on a string. Sphinx glugs it back.

I tan I epi tas.

Moon I tan I what?

Sphinx I tan I epi tas. A toast.

Moon What's it mean?

Sphinx I tan I epi tas? With your shield or on it. The Spartan women say it to their sons and husbands and they off to their clodhopper wars.

Moon They love their wars.

Sphinx As do we.

Moon I tan I epi tas.

Raising her glass.

Sphinx Yeah.

Raising the bottle.
Lights.

Act Two

Darkness to shadow. Women singing a lament as they process across the stage. A funeral procession of women. Polynices on his shield is carried by the women mourners. All in black except for Polynices who is wrapped in a white shroud.

Women
My proud warrior.
My gorgeous flower.
My cypress tree.
Your voice deeper
Than any other.
Why bless us with sons
For the ferryman.
Stealing them
Across the silver river
In their prime.
How lovely you were
At the feast.
Whirling in the dance.
The olive branch leaned
Down to you.
Deer ate from your hand.
Wild boar feared you.
And young girls put
Garlands in your hair.
Proud son of proud Oedipus
And straight-backed Jocasta.
The Gods marked you
From the cradle.

Now they take you home
To the land of pomegranate.
The gardens of asphodel
Watered by the five rivers
And the tears of the dead . . .

Creon has entered with soldiers. The women see him and gradually stop singing.

Creon Antigone.

Antigone Uncle.

Creon What's the meaning of this?

Antigone Isn't it obvious?

Creon (*examining corpse*) Polynices?

Antigone What's left of him.

Creon What did I say?

Antigone You know what you said.

Creon Tell me.

Antigone That he's not to be buried.

Creon What else?

Antigone That he's to be left rot where he fell.

Creon What else?

Antigone That anyone who removes his corpse does so on pain of death.

Creon Do you understand what that means?

Antigone Stop talking down to me.

Creon And you dare defy me?

Antigone He's my brother.

Creon He's a traitor.

Antigone I know but he's still my brother.

Creon He came against his own. His own people. Have you seen the carnage?

Antigone I have.

Creon The slaughter?

Antigone Yes Uncle I've seen it.

Creon There's hardly a young man left alive. I'm ruling a city of widows and orphans. My son is dead. Megareus. He died defending this city.

Antigone I'm sorry about Megareus.

Creon Then why this?

Antigone I'm sorry for it all.

Creon Your mother is dead.

Antigone My women told me. Topped herself.

Creon That's right. Threw herself off Sphinx crag when she saw what this traitor, this savage has done. And now you want to bury him. Why add to her shame?

Antigone How am I adding to her shame?

Creon You know well how.

Antigone By defying you?

Creon By defying the laws of this city.

Antigone Which is you now.

Creon Which is me now. Are you aware this cutthroat you want to bury killed Eteocles? His own brother? Your brother?

Antigone I heard they killed each other.

Creon And that doesn't shock you?

Antigone I'm beyond shock.

Creon What happened to your father?

Antigone I don't know.

Creon What do you mean you don't know? Is he dead or alive?

Antigone He disappeared.

Creon He can't have just disappeared.

Antigone I found his clothes.

Creon No other trace? No body?

Antigone No. He wouldn't even give us that.

Creon This is what you're going to do. You're going to retrace your steps and dump that treacherous runt back in the field where you found him. You hear me? And we'll say no more about it. You're my sister's child. I'm your Godfather. You're not thinking straight. None of us are and how could we be? Go on. Before I change my mind.

Antigone I can't.

Creon You can't?

Antigone I'm not leaving him for the wolf and the crow.

Creon I'm not asking. I'm ordering.

Antigone You just left him there. You refused him the surgeons, a drop of water, a word of comfort. How could you?

Creon I refused him nothing. It was madness here in the thick of the fray. He was gone by the time I found him.

Antigone You're supposed to be in charge and you let them mutilate him. My brother. I had to gather him in bits and pieces. So many wounds I can't count them. A lump of seething meat, his skin hanging off, blades, rocks, the boot. You allowed this.

Creon I didn't allow it.

Antigone You didn't stop it.

Creon I told you they got to him before I did but he deserved every blow, taunt, jeer, he got after what he's done. He came against his own with the Argives and you know what their tactics are. No quarter given, not to women, not even to children. He had that savage death coming to him and we're not burying him.

Antigone Everyone deserves a grave Creon.

Creon No they don't. No they do not. My rule now. My laws.

Antigone Well if you're talking rule and law I'm the rightful ruler of Thebes now.

Creon You?

Antigone My mother, father, brothers gone. I'm the next in direct line.

Creon You don't know your genealogy girl. My line is as direct as yours. I ruled this city alongside your mother and I ruled it well until your father comes limping to my palace door saying he's the new king, crowned by the Sphinx, carrying parchments from Delphi, covering all his bases the scheming thug, announcing from the rooftops he's come to save us all.

Antigone And save you he did.

Creon And your mother wakes out of her two-decade sleep and is in thrall. Never seen anything like it, the single-minded obsession of it.

Antigone She didn't know. How could she have?

Creon Wake up girl. She knew. We all knew. The big open secret and we let it go until he gets it into his head to bring the big open secret into the open.

Antigone Everyone knows it was you did that. You saw your chance. You pounced. And now you think you see your chance again. You think to take this city from me? To leave my brother, son of Oedipus, without shroud or burial? You think to leave him like the carcass of a beast on the side of the hill. I don't think so.

Creon How dare you talk down to me? Give me orders? Over my dead body will you put him in hallowed ground with the sacred honours we reserve for the faithful.

Antigone He'd never have come against Thebes if you'd given him his due. Polynices loved this land. It was his turn to rule. But you couldn't control him the way you could Eteocles. You have your plan to be rid of us all. I've watched you. You think a girl can't watch. Well this girl is the rightful ruler of Thebes by all the laws of this city going back to Cadmus and his serpent bride Harmonia. And by the laws of this city I will put my brother into the earth where he belongs. Back into Demeter's cold brown arms. Everyone deserves that. Who do you think you are to defy me and defy the rules of eternity? We are Hades' children, on brief loan from our first breath. Your fanatic heart and bullnecked stupidity blinds you to who rules the world.

Creon I rule the world. This bit of it. The Gods can have the rest.

Antigone The Gods rule all and they're raging at your crimes.

Creon My crimes?

Antigone You've destroyed my family. Taking us out one by one.

Creon Wasn't me destroyed your family. It was your pigheaded father lusting after his own mother. And before that it was your paedophile grandfather. Between the lot of you, you've brought this great city to its knees and I'm only sorry I didn't step in sooner. Law is law and your family has broken every one of them. No longer. I'm putting things to right and you will submit to the law of this land.

Antigone I am the law of this land by all the rights of inheritance handed down since time immemorial.

Creon You want to die? You want me to do it for you? You want a martyr's glory? Lay and legend singing your sorry praises down the ages?

Antigone I want to do what's right?

Creon And the rest of us are doing what's wrong?

Antigone The kingship of this city is my concern. Where my brother's bones rest is my concern. I spit on your savage laws that go against the people and mock the rule of heaven.

Creon You going to give me a sermon from your pulpit now? A lecture on ethics? What are you the high priest of Delphi?

Antigone Something much lower than that uncle. I'm the Queen of Thebes.

Creon The Queen of Thebes.

Antigone You slunk in on my mother's coattails after Laius was murdered. You have no legitimate claim to my father's crown, my mother's, my brothers', mine. And after me my children will rule this city.

Creon What children? You'll have to have them first. You'll have to marry first. You'll have to be left alive first.
   (*To the soldiers, indicating corpse of Polynices.*) Remove that treacherous bastard from my sight.

Antigone Don't you lay a hand on him!

Soldiers freeze.

Creon Move! Put him back where she found him!

Antigone If you dare!

Creon Oh I dare. Better still fling him on the dungheap . . .

Antigone Do not touch my brother!

Creon The battlefield too good for him. Let slurry and sewer be his grave.

Antigone (*going for Creon*) I'll dig him up and bury him again and then I'll drown you in that sewer.

Women moving in as Antigone and Creon struggle. Soldiers frozen over Polynices' body, not sure who to obey.

Creon (*holding Antigone in a vice grip*) Stay back!
You're hot on the boil and I'm out of grace with you.

Antigone wallops him, he wallops her back.

You know your problem little niece, little godchild, you don't know when to put a door on your mouth.

Clamps his hand over her mouth.

Your bolshy talk is wind and water to try and sway the people. I don't see them swaying. You know why? Because they know full well where the curse of Oedipus and his tainted brood has brought us to. This ravaged city of weeping mothers and orphans all because of your father's arrogant crimes and your mother's filthy marriage bed and your brother's at each other's throats like blinded rats. All without a thought for the cost to Thebes and Thebans. And still you have the gall to stand here and pontificate about your rights and your Gods as if you know them. No one knows the Gods. And least of all a deluded upstart girl.

Antigone No delusion I assure you Uncle. To live in the mystery of our lives. To die in the mystery. Believing in the mystery. This is our purpose. Not to be seduced by the fallible decrees of despots and tyrants. Not to buckle

under the spite and evil of monsters who make their laws
on the hoof for personal gain. They walked among us once.
They made us in their image. They taught us the first laws.
The blood laws. We know them in our bowels. Laws that
are the touchstone of our race, the memory of our ancient
beginnings and immortal longings. These things happened.
These beings exist. Realer than us. They are here still. And
the dead are here too, wailing from their pits. Listen, they
cry, do not do as I did. Do not forget the insane miracle that
is your brief sojourn before you swoon back down the stairs
of time into the arms of the void. Our lives are arrows aimed
at the dark. Phantoms in the making, scavengers of the land,
when we should be souls standing tall in the blessed finery
of skin and limb and thought, our hearts stamped with the
imprint of Olympus before its golden gates clanged on our
exiled backs. There is home. Not here. There is our first and
true home. Not here. And it is the dictates of there I obey
first. Not you and this desecration, this gobbledygook you
dare to call the law. Hunted and haunted I may be but I am
sure of one thing. The Gods' glorious dream for us. And it is
glorious. And I will honour it whatever the price. I will bury
my brother though it cost me my life.

Creon Then go to your dream you sorrow-drenched rip.
Down with you to Hades' house where the walls are black
as the sloe. Where the dead weep for the light up here.
Blessed Boetian light. Away with her to the old tomb where
they say the sown men are buried and you can converse
with their bones to your hearts content.

All look at him.

I said take her away!
   All of you!
   Go!

*All exit, soldiers with Polynices. Other soldiers with
Antigone, procession of women. Haimon entering as
Antigone exits.*

Haimon Antigone . . . I'm sorry about your mother, your brothers.

Antigone My father . . . They're all gone Haimon.

Haimon What's happening here?

Antigone I was burying Polynices.

Haimon But you heard the decree?

Antigone I did. Can you bury him for me? My last wish before the God of Death puts me to bed.

And the soldiers rush her off followed by the procession.

Haimon Wait. What?

Looks at Creon.

What have you done?

Creon What I had to.

Haimon You're going to have her killed for throwing a few handfuls of clay over her brother?

Creon She knew the penalty.

Haimon But this is Antigone. My cousin. Your niece. Your sister's daughter. I'm marrying her come spring.

Creon The King of the Dead is her groom now.

Haimon You can't do this.

Creon The girl is mad. The taint is in her. Do you want children from that blood line?

Haimon That's not her fault. Did she ask to be born to them?

Creon She flaunts it, flouts it, throws it in our faces when she should be hiding away in shame.

Haimon There's been enough death around here.

Creon That's for sure.

Haimon You haven't mourned Megareus.

Creon I'll mourn him when I've time to bloody mourn.

Haimon You barely sat through the funeral. My mother is wailing at his grave. Go to her.

Creon She won't let me near her.

Haimon She has her reasons.

Creon What's that supposed to mean?

Haimon You could've called this war off and well you know it.

Creon I did everything I could to stop it.

Haimon Not what they're saying on the ground.

Creon What are they saying?

Haimon They're saying it's all gone as planned. They're saying, look who's wearing the crown. They're angry, vengeful, out for blood, waiting for any excuse to turn. And now this? Antigone? This is going too far. This will do it.

Creon Let them try and they'll find I'm out for blood too.

Haimon She's a defenceless girl. Daughter of the great Oedipus.

Creon The great Oedipus? That their tune now? Let them say what they like so long as they do what they're told.

Haimon They'll say she's in the right to bury him and you know it's the right thing too. What possessed you to pass such a decree? Imagine if that was Megareus? His poor mangled body left in the field?

Creon I'll lose face if I climb down.

Haimon You won't.

Creon As it is we're holding on by a thread.

Haimon We? Leave me out of this. Are you out of your mind thinking I want any part in this?

Creon Are you going to cross me too?

Haimon What I'm saying is, it's better to be clement, merciful, just. The people always respect that.

Creon This is justice! Justice for those who were slaughtered because of him. This is justice for my brave Megareus. And as for clemency, it's for the weak, the vanquished, the ones who don't count. The dregs who'll never rule. Clemency, Mercy, Kindness, these are the luxuries of the low, the feeble, the women. And I won't be made a jackass of over a woman. Not even a woman, a girl, a scheming, vindictive, entitled little girl bitch, arguing with me like a man. In front of the whole city. No sir, she's getting what she deserves.

Haimon If you let her die they'll turn. I'm telling you they'll take you down.

Creon I have the army to keep them in line.

Haimon The army won't stand by and let you kill Oedipus' daughter.

Creon They are. They will.

Haimon Then let her go, for my sake.

Creon I'm doing this for you as much as me. She's too unpredictable, too much of a hot head, too much of everything. She'll stir up trouble at every turn. Better this way. Haimon, you're young and the world is full of willing girls. You'll have the pick of them. You're the King's last living son. You'll rule Thebes after me.

Haimon (*exiting*) You're a staggering fool.

Creon What did you say?

Haimon Fit you better to go and tend my heartbroken mother instead of this skulduggery.

Creon I'm warning you do not interfere!

Haimon This is your kingship is it? This is how you mean to start your reign? On the bones of a grief stricken girl?

Creon I'm warning you. A father's warning. Not a king's. Don't cross me over Antigone. She has you by the balls. You want them saying you were cornered by a girl. There is Law Haimon and then there is women.

Haimon It's no disgrace to obey a woman when she's in the right. It's no disgrace to back down.

Creon So now you're going to tell me how to rule?

Haimon This decree is insane.

Creon Insane?

Haimon The whole city says it.

Creon You talk to your father like this? Your king?

Haimon You're no king.

Creon You want me to drag her back? Cut her head off in front of you?
   Here? Now?

Haimon If you kill her you'll kill me.

Creon Enough with the high talk.

Haimon I won't allow it.

Creon And how will you stop it?

Haimon You'll never set eyes on me again.

Exit Haimon.

Creon Get back here! Haimon! Haimon!

The Shee has entered.

The Shee Kick the girl when she's down.

Creon God almighty am I never to be free of you hovering and spying?

The Shee Your son gives good advice. Let her go. Let her bury her brother.

Creon Get out of here.

The Shee The Sphinx is on Cithaeron again breathing her fumes of blight over the land. The Dark Destroyers are on the hunt. The Watchers from the other side, moving in.

Creon Aren't they always?

The Shee Oh the big man in his big crown. They'll batter the pride and arrogance out of you before sundown. They're coming for you and nothing surer.

Creon Let them come. I passed a law. A just law. I upheld it. You think I want the girl dead?

The Shee More than the girl will die.

Creon What are you saying?

The Shee You'll pay blood for blood.

Creon Who?

The Shee The Gods are particular when it comes to revenge.

Creon She broke the law.

The Shee And obeyed the higher one.

Creon I told the soldiers to leave food and water when they wall her in. I'll release her when she cools off, submits to me, behaves herself.

The Shee You think it wise to leave a proud doomed girl walled in stone? In the dark? Grieving for all the ones she lost? No hope. I heard you. You gave orders for her death.

Creon To put manners on her.

The Shee She doesn't know that.

Creon You think she'll harm herself?

The Shee I think you play fast and loose with sacred laws.

Creon (*to soldier*) Bring Antigone to me. At once.

The Shee The fear of the God is in you now and not before time.

Creon Polynices.

The Shee What about him?

Creon Should I relent? Allow the burial?

The Shee You have to ask that question?

Creon I'll bury him with all the honours. Will that satisfy your Oracles?

Enter Haimon carrying the dead Antigone. Music to accompany.

Creon Haimon.

Haimon You did this.

Creon I only meant to frighten her . . .
   (*To soldiers.*) I told you to watch her.
   Did I not give orders to keep her close? Haimon . . .
it wasn't meant to go this way . . .
   I just sent a soldier to release her.

Haimon I begged you.

Puts Antigone down. Runs at Creon with a knife. Soldiers stop him.

I told you what would happen!
   I told you.

Creon (*to soldiers*) Let him go.
I said let him go.

Haimon with knife to Creon's throat.

Haimon . . . I was wrong . . . this war . . . don't do this. Not like Oedipus . . . a father's blood . . . that awful curse on yourself . . . on all of us . . . I'll bury Polynices. I'll bury them together. Brother and sister. A big funeral.

Haimon You won't.

Creon I swear I will.

Haimon You won't.

Creon I will. I will

Haimon Do what you want now.

Slits his own throat, reels, falls on top of Antigone. No one moves.
Silence.

The Shee Take them away.
Prepare them for the Earth.

Soldiers carry off Antigone and Haimon.

Creon Take me away too . . . out of everyone's sight.

The Shee There's more.

Creon What more? My sons are dead. What more can there be woman? Where's my wife? I have to tell her. Where's Eurydice? How am I to bring her this news? Her last living child.

A wail offstage.

The Shee She knows. Listen. Her women are telling her that Haimon is dead.

Silence.

Gone. She's gone too. Don't say you weren't warned. How the ones above balance the books. But who listens to the Shee? Who ever has?

Creon No! No! No!

Creon runs off.

The Shee Wait. One last message from the Oracle.

Unrolls a golden parchment. Reads. Music.

Tell your king, my hall has fallen. No longer have I a hut, nor a prophetic laurel. The water has dried up. My voice is stilled.

She rolls up the scroll. Looks out. Exits.

Act Three

SCENE 1

Music. Voices. Out of the darkness as if from a great distance. Crackle. Planetary wind. Music.

Jocasta Hello . . . hello.

Woman Hello.

Jocasta Hello.

Woman Yes I'm here.

Silence.

Jocasta Where's the blood?

Woman I have it.

Jocasta Then pour.

Sound of blood pouring, sound of Jocasta drinking, amplified. A huge gasp from Jocasta.

Woman Is it okay?

Jocasta More. More.

Repeat of pouring and drinking, gasp etc.

Jocasta Aaah! Warm. Good. Is it yours?

Woman No it's not mine. Is it enough.

Jocasta Never enough.

Woman Can we speak now?

Jocasta It was all so long ago.

Woman How long?

Jocasta I've lost track of time here. Let me see. Twelve thousand years I'd say give or take.

Woman That long?

Jocasta Thereabouts. That's when it was spoken about. But I think the story is as old as the first people who sat round the fire in the cave.

Woman What was it like then?

Jocasta When I lived? Or back in the cave?

Woman Both. Either.

Jocasta I never lived in a cave.

Woman Then what was it like when you lived?

Jocasta In Thebes?

Woman Yeah. What was the world like then?

Jocasta Glorious.

Lights up, dome of sky, stars, moons, planets, what galaxy is this?

Woman Glorious?

Jocasta Anywhere is glorious from here.

Woman Jocasta isn't it? They said your name is Jocasta.

Jocasta That's right.

Woman Mother of Oedipus?

Jocasta You've heard of Oedipus?

Woman I have.

Jocasta Have you seen him?

Woman No. Have you?

Jocasta Not since Colonus. Not since he floated away.

Woman Did that really happen?

Jocasta They said it did. I wasn't there.

Woman Is it true you were married to him?

Jocasta Why do you want to know?

Woman Is it true?

Jocasta It is.

Woman Your son?

Jocasta He was.

Woman What was that like?

Jocasta Everyone wants to know that.

Woman Must've been strange.

Jocasta For others.

Woman Not for you?

Jocasta Not for me. Not for him. Not when it was just us.

Woman What did you do?

Jocasta What do you mean what did we do?

Woman When you were alone?

Jocasta Ah . . . we did everything.

Woman Everything?

Jocasta And we did it well. My husband was king.

Woman Was he a good king?

Jocasta The best.

Woman Good to the people?

Jocasta Too good.

Woman The slaves?

Jocasta How can you be good to slaves? It's a contradiction isn't it? How can you be good to someone you own body and soul? Do you have slaves where you come from?

Woman We do.

Jocasta Then don't ask stupid questions. But to answer you, my husband, my son, treated most people badly.

Woman And you?

Jocasta I was a paragon.

Woman I doubt that.

Jocasta What is it you want?

Woman You drank the blood. You tell the truth. That's the oath.

Jocasta Ah the truth.

Woman Your children?

Jocasta The beautiful children.

Woman Polynices, Eteocles, Antigone, Ismene.

Jocasta You know I hardly remember them. The odd flash and they fade again.

Woman All of them were with your son? With Oedipus?

Jocasta If you say so.

Woman Must've been odd for them. Did they know?

Jocasta No secrets in Thebes.

Woman What did they make of you and Oedipus?

Jocasta They loved us. They had no choice but to love us.

Woman Did you have a favourite child?

Jocasta No.

Woman That's not what has come down.

Jocasta I don't care what has come down. You're asking me. I'm telling you. I loved all my children the same. But . . .

Woman But?

Jocasta I worried about him more.

Woman Oedipus?

Jocasta Oedipus.

Woman Why?

Jocasta Why do you think?

Woman He was damaged.

Jocasta We're all damaged.

Woman You put him on the mountain. Cithaeron. Nailed to an oak tree.

Jocasta It was an olive tree.

Woman An olive tree.

Jocasta Laius did that.

Woman Some say it was you.

Jocasta Of course they did. If in doubt blame the mother.

Woman What really happened?

Jocasta So long ago. He was three days old. They took him.

Woman You handed him over.

Jocasta I didn't fight hard enough.

Woman Because of the curse?

Jocasta I don't believe in curses.

Woman They say you handed him over. That it was common enough at the time.

Jocasta It was. Famine after famine. Plague. Never enough to go round. Women had huge families. If you married at fourteen you could have thirty children. I knew women who had. What's one nailed to a tree if you have thirty?

Woman So it was normal enough?

Jocasta You had to put them on the mountain before they were ten days old. After ten days it was considered too cruel.

Woman Why ten days?

Jocasta Because by ten days mother and baby would be inseparable. The hills were full of women hiding out with new-borns. If you got them to ten days they couldn't take them off you.

Woman Was that a law?

Jocasta I should've taken to the hills.

Woman Why didn't you?

Jocasta There was no need. He was my first. He was a boy. My husband was the king. I didn't have thirty children. I didn't see it coming. I woke and he wasn't in his cot. They took him.

Woman And then you got him back.

Jocasta And then I got him back.

Woman That must've been something.

Jocasta For a time. For a long time. Those were the years.

Woman What do you mean?

Jocasta You know damn well what I mean.

Woman Then what happened?

Jocasta What usually happens.

Woman Did you know all along?

Jocasta That he was my son? Of course I knew.

Woman How did you know?

Jocasta The serpent's mark.

Woman The what?

Jocasta The serpent's mark. We all had it. The Cadmean line. A gift from Harmonia, Cadmus' serpent queen. We all had it. Tattooed on our skin as we slipped from the womb.

Uncovers herself.

There's mine. Oedipus's was on his back. Same with Polynices and Eteocles. The girls. Antigone, her arm. Ismene, the left thigh.

Woman And Oedipus would have known too?

Jocasta Sure he knew.

Woman And still?

Jocasta Read the old stories. They're full of it.

Woman An obsession then?

Jocasta It never felt like that.

Woman How did it feel?

Jocasta It felt right.

Woman Even when you knew?

Jocasta That made it clearer.

Woman How so?

Jocasta You don't love a stranger like that.

Woman A stranger?

Jocasta Like a husband. A husband is a stranger isn't he? Isn't that what he's meant to be? By law?

Woman One way of looking at it.

Jocasta Anyone who isn't your blood is a stranger.

Woman I suppose.

Jocasta Is it different now?

Woman Not really.

Jocasta It's always frowned upon. You're stirring up memories . . . things I haven't thought about in . . .

Woman You lived as husband and wife until the end?

Jocasta We were married a long time. Desire comes and goes.

Woman But desire was there?

Jocasta The bond was there.

Woman What sort of bond? Mother bond? Son bond? Natural bond? Unnatural?

Jocasta We come from the animal kingdom and maybe the first star and who can say what is natural and unnatural. You put too much emphasis on me being his mother.

Woman Do I?

Jocasta Are you a bit of a prude?

Woman I'm fascinated.

Jocasta I understand fascination. We fascinated ourselves. A huge part of the attraction. But the thing that upended everything was that he killed his father.

Woman I was coming to that.

Jocasta I was married to a murderer. That was the shock. The hardest to stomach.

Woman But you hated Laius.

Jocasta Did I?

Woman I thought . . .

Jocasta He didn't want to marry me. Chrysippus was the one he loved.

Woman The boy?

Jocasta Yeah the boy.

Woman Was that usual then?

Jocasta Men and boys? It was an epidemic. Laius's crime wasn't that he raped the boy. It was that he raped him without his father's permission. He broke the rules of hospitality, didn't ask for Chrysippus with the appropriate gift price. He stole him and then he refused to give him back.

Woman Fathers handed their sons over to men?

Jocasta And mothers. If it was to the family's advantage. Happened all the time. Can't imagine that has changed has it?

Woman We call it different names now. It's more furtive.

Jocasta It was done openly in my day.

Woman You weren't jealous of this boy?

Jocasta Jealous of a child?

Woman You were happy to have him in your house?

Jocasta My father had many boys. I was used to it.

Woman What happened to Chrysippus?

Jocasta I don't want to talk anymore about Chrysippus.

Woman Why not?

Jocasta Because he's the reason I'm here. He's the reason I'm damned.

Woman What did you do to him?

Jocasta That was my crime. Not marrying my son. Not the steaming incestuous sheets. Not all the inbred children who went before me to their graves.

Woman Is that what they said to you?

Jocasta That's what I say to myself.

Woman Is it true you hanged yourself?

Jocasta Twice.

Woman How do you hang yourself twice?

Jocasta The first time Oedipus cut me down.

Woman After they found out he was your son?

Jocasta After I found out he was a murderer.

Woman And the second time?

Jocasta When they killed my daughters.
Antigone and Ismene.

Woman Who killed them?

Jocasta My brother.

Woman Creon?

Jocasta You've heard of him?

Woman To kill his own nieces? Why?

Jocasta Any number of reasons. Take your pick.

Woman I thought it was because of Polynices.

Jocasta What about Polynices?

Woman Didn't Antigone bury Polynices against Creon's wishes?

Jocasta I buried Polynices.

Woman Oh?

Jocasta I buried him with Eteocles. I had to put them in the one grave they were that stuck together. Like ivy. Clinging to each other. I buried them. I don't know where you're getting your information from.

Woman But it's a famous story.

Jocasta What is?

Woman Antigone burying Polynices. Defying Creon. Creon walling her up in a tomb alive. A girl at war with the state. It's one of the great myths of civilisation.

Jocasta Ah the great myths of civilisation. Never happened. I buried my sons. Just like the Shee said. All gone. All gone. End of the line.

Woman All of them?

Jocasta In two days.

Woman You must've lost your mind.

Jocasta It's still lost.

Woman And Oedipus? Did he really disappear into thin air or is that another tale?

Jocasta The only reason I agreed to talk to you was they said you have news of him.

Woman I don't. I'm sorry.

Jocasta Is he a God in your world?

Woman More a cautionary tale.

Jocasta And what am I? Don't tell me. A martyr?

Woman They say the grief killed you.

Jocasta Well that much is true.

Woman They don't like that you might have lived.

Jocasta Might have? I lived. I lived it all.

Woman They want you spotless. Innocent.

Jocasta They want me ignorant. A blubbering moron. A blameless fool.

Woman Whatever way you look at it, it's not right.

Jocasta Mother and son? Maybe it isn't but it happens.

Lights.

SCENE 2

Music. Enter Oedipus in white flowing robes. No limp. Eyes perfect. Beautiful light. Enter Queen of the Furies.

Queen F Settling in okay?

Oedipus Getting used to it.

Queen F They looking after you?

Oedipus They are.

Queen F Anything you need just let them know.

Oedipus It's a bit isolated.

Queen F That's for your safety.

Oedipus Am I in danger?

Queen F I've told them to let you have the use of my garden.

Oedipus I hear voices behind the wall.

Queen F The place is teeming.

Oedipus And at night the screeching and wailing.

Queen F The damned on their way.

Oedipus On their way where?

Queen F Where do you think? Food's okay?

Oedipus Excellent.

Queen F The leg?

Oedipus Perfect.

Queen F Good. And your eyes?

Oedipus Sight restored. Did you arrange that?

Queen F How did you lose your sight?

Oedipus One minute I see, the next I'm blind.

Queen F Just like that?

Oedipus Pretty much.

Queen F I heard different.

Oedipus What did you hear?

Queen F You did it yourself.

Oedipus What is this? What do you want?

Queen F Just curious. Before the judgement.

Oedipus Judgement?

Queen F Yeah.

Oedipus All my life I've been judged. Nothing I did was ever good enough, right enough. I thought I was done with all that.

Queen F Can you remember what happened?

Oedipus Of course I can remember what happened.

Queen F Then tell me why you blinded yourself.

Oedipus It's a private matter.

Queen F You couldn't look anymore? At yourself?

Oedipus At the world.

Queen F You were going to kill yourself.

Oedipus What is this?

Queen F But that wouldn't have fed the big ego. The big destiny. That would've made them too happy. And you've never been into other people's happiness.

Oedipus Happiness is for children.

Queen F They say you blinded yourself to stay king.

Oedipus They say all sorts when you're king.

Queen F Is this the knife you used?

Oedipus Where did you get that?

Queen F The same knife you used to kill your father.

Oedipus What of it?

Queen F I'm trying to help you out here.

Oedipus It's just a knife.

Queen F Do you regret it?

Oedipus Regret what?

Queen F Your father?

Oedipus What use is regret?

Queen F Tell me about Colonus?

Oedipus It was amazing.

Queen F Your death?

Oedipus I was right. All along I was right.

Queen F It's important for you to be right?

Oedipus On this yes. My whole life I carried this stain, this mark, this taint, but I also carried something beautiful and mysterious. My death proved that.

Queen F Proved what?

Oedipus My name will be there forever. What I suffered. What I learned. This is how you become a God.

Queen F A God? You?

Oedipus You still doubt me? The Oracle said.

Queen F Phoebus Apollo?

Oedipus From his own lips.

Queen F That psychopath? That parvenu? That trumped up woman hating runt of the first order. You backed the wrong God.

Oedipus What are you saying? Who are you? The Oracle said . . .

Queen F Ah the Oracle. He makes it up as he goes along. You messed with my grave.

Oedipus I messed with no grave.

Queen F At Colonus.

Oedipus That old tomb?

Queen F My old tomb.

Oedipus You're mistaken. That old tomb belonged to the Furies.

Queen F That's right.

Oedipus They're gone. They've been gone forever.

Queen F Do I look gone to you?

Oedipus Who are you?

Queen F I'm the Queen of the Furies and I judge blood crime.

Oedipus Where am I?

Queen F Where did you think you were? Paradise with your little Gods?

Are you afraid?

Oedipus Should I be?

Queen F There's someone wants to meet you.

Oedipus Jocasta?

Queen F Come in!

Enter Laius. Music. They stand looking at one another.

Laius Son.

End.